# OLD WITHERIDGE

## BYGONE DAYS IN A DEVON VILLAGE

Compiled by
John Usmar and Peter and Freda Tout

DEVON BOOKS

First published in Great Britain in 1988 by Devon Books

**British Library Cataloguing-in-Publication Data**

Old Witheridge : a portrait of a Devon
   village.
   1. Witheridge (Devon) — History
   2. Witheridge (Devon) — Description — Views
   I. Usmar, John II. Tout, Peter III. Tout,
   Freda
   942.3'54      DA690.W81/

ISBN 0-86114-821-5

Printed and bound in Great Britain by A. Wheaton & Co. Ltd

DEVON BOOKS
**Official Publisher to Devon County Council**
An imprint of Wheaton Publishers Ltd, a member of
Pergamon/BPCC Publishing Corporation PLC

Wheaton Publishers Ltd
Hennock Road, Marsh Barton, Exeter, Devon EX2 8RP
Tel: 0392 74121; Telex 42794 (WHEATN G)

SALES
Direct sales enquiries to Devon Books at the address above.
Trade Sales to: Town & Country Books, P.O. Box 31, Newton Abbot,
Devon TQ12 5AQ. Tel: 080 47 2690

*Front cover picture:* Witheridge Fair before 1914

# INTRODUCTION

The village of Witheridge lies halfway between Tiverton and South Molton on the border between North and Mid Devon. Much of the Parish lies at around 600ft above sea level, and the countryside consists mainly of rolling farmland cut by the valleys of the Little Dart River and the Adworthy, Sturcombe and Fulford streams, together with Witheridge and Darte Raffe Moors. It was these moors that saw the first settlements some 3000 years ago, and the Bronze Age burial mounds on the two moors are evidence of this. The climate was drier then, and a living was to be made on the higher ground, while the valleys were still choked with tree growth.

Fifteen hundred years later there was an immigration of Celtic peoples, bringing their new Iron Age technology, and this, with a wetter climate, stirred them into clearing some of the forests and extending the area available for cultivation. They have left the Celtic river-name 'Dart', as a reminder of their presence.

The Romans made little impact on this part of Devon, but it may be that the turmoil following their departure caused local people to build the earthwork known as Berry Castle near Higher Queen Dart, as a place of refuge.

By 900AD Witheridge was important enough to have given its name to the 'Hundred', which is one of the largest in Devon and contains such Parishes as Cruwys Morchard, Rackenford, Bishopsnympton, Kingsnympton and Chulmleigh. When the Domesday record was made there were twelve identifiable manors within the present Parish boundaries, with another twenty-five holdings not named, so it is possible that very nearly all today's farm sites were established before 1086. In those days scribes wrote down the names of places as they thought they heard people say them, so there was Wiriga, Wetherigge, Wytherigge and many other versions. It is likely that it is an 'Old English' name simply meaning 'ridge of the wethers', which indicates the importance of sheep then.

By 1550 Witheridge had become a Borough with a market, fair and Court of the Duchy of Lancaster, but Borough status had lapsed by the end of the eighteenth century, probably due to nearby towns proving more central and more popular. In 1840, a direct turnpike was opened from South Molton through Witheridge to Tiverton. At that time the village was self-supporting in most things, and the Directories of the nineteenth and early twentieth centuries show a complete range of shops and services. But better communications were one factor that led to a slow decline in population from 1,340 in 1841 (including perhaps 50 in outlying parts of the Parish later hived off to neighbouring Parishes), to 670 in 1971, whence it rose to 1,100 in 1987. Agriculture was always important locally, and continues to be so, but with fewer jobs on the land, many now find other employment either locally or in nearby towns.

We have had two aims in putting this book together; firstly to preserve some of the history of Witheridge between about 1880 and 1950, and secondly to produce something of value to residents and visitors alike. We have had a marvellous response from people with photographs, postcards and memories, and we thank them; if there are any omitted from our list we offer them our apologies. We have done our best to check our information in the captions and regret any errors that may have crept in. One or two of the photographs are not of the standard that we would have liked, but because of their particular interest we have included them. The quotation marks in the captions indicate the actual words used by those who shared their memories with us.

We hope this book will bring interest and enjoyment to many people.

John Usmar, Peter and Freda Tout

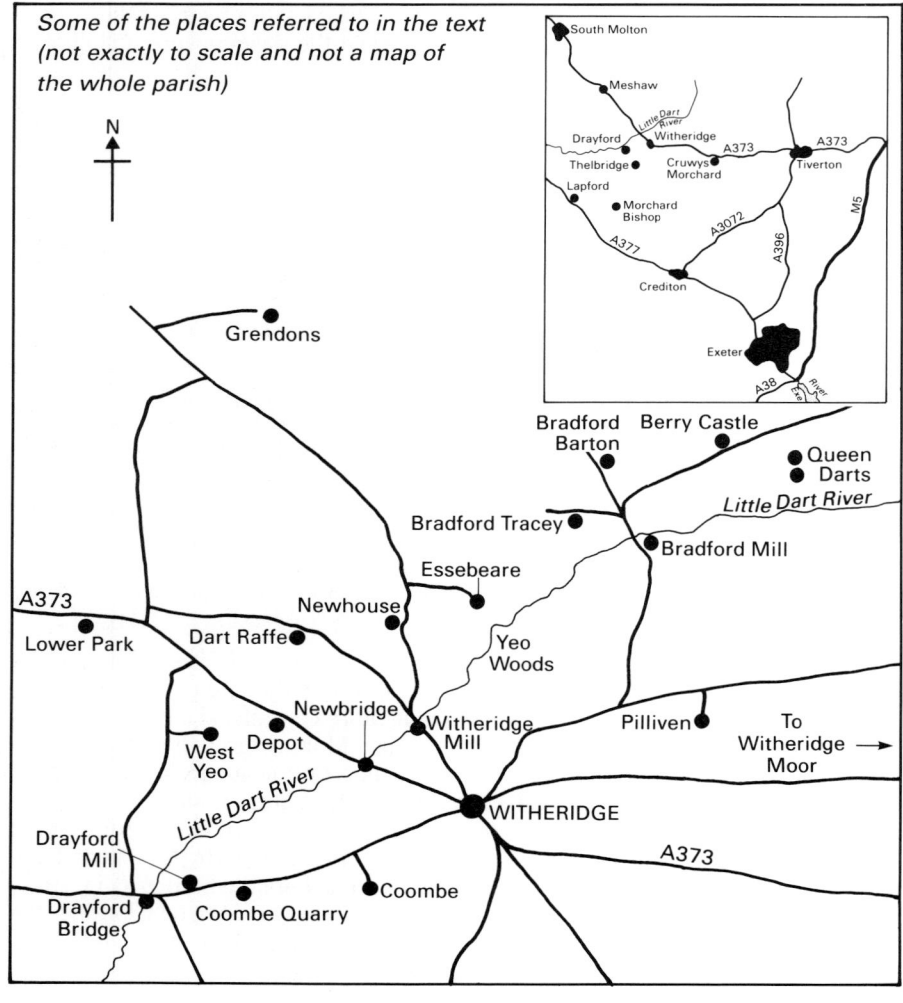

Some of the places referred to in the text (not exactly to scale and not a map of the whole parish)

Parish maps

4

**WITHERIDGE** is a parish and village on the road from South Molton to Tiverton, 7 miles north-east from Lapford station on the North Devon branch of the London and South Western railway, and about 8 south-east from Bishopsnympton station on the Barnstaple section of the Great Western railway, 10½ south-east from South Molton and 10½ west-by-north from Tiverton, in the Northern division of the county, Witheridge hundred, South Molton petty sessional division, union and county court district, and in the rural deanery of South Molton, archdeaconry of Barnstaple and diocese of Exeter. The church of St. John the Baptist is an edifice of stone in the Early Perpendicular style.

### PRIVATE RESIDENTS.

Adams William, The Square
Bennett Thomas, North street
Benson Rev. John Peter M.A. (vicar & rural dean), Vicarage
Benson Miss E. The Lawn
Charlton Thomas William, Colleton hall, Hill town
Cheney Rev. Henry (Congregational), The Manse
Cock George, Commercial cottage
Cutcliffe Mrs. Coombe house
Elworthy Mrs. Lashbrook
Fernie Miss, The Square
Folland Frank, Burn house
Holt Geo. Frederick, Lawn cottage
Partridge Mrs. Elizabeth, Fern cot
Partridge Mrs. Ellen, South street
Pullen Geo. Henry, sen. Rosemont vil
Shelley Percy Wilfred Graham M.R.C.S.Eng., L.R.C.P.Lond. Cypress house
Tucker Mrs. Fore street

### COMMERCIAL.

Adams Richard, dairyman, The Lawn
Adams Richard, farmer, Hole
Addicott Fanny (Mrs.), nurse
Alford William, blacksmith, West st
Ayre George Thomas, farmer, Lower Queendart
Ayre Michael, farmer, Downe
Ayre Thomas, farmer, Witheridge moor
Baker Charles, dairyman, Litterbarn
Baker William, blacksmith
Bennett Harriet (Miss), shopkeeper, Fore street
Bennett James, shoe maker, Fore st
Besley Henry, farmer, East Piliven
Blackford Henry, miller (water), Bradford mill
Board Thos. farmer, Higher Adworthy
Bodley Thos. carpenter, Pullen's row
Boundy Frederick, farmer, Horestone
Bowden Robt. jobbing grdnr. Gunn hole
Bowden Robt. jun. mason, Gunn hole
Bradford Wm. chimney swpr. Penford
Bucknell Robert, farmer, Westeria ho
Bulled Edmund, wheelwright, The Square
Bulled John, dog trainer
Burnett Ann (Miss), dress ma. West st
Chapple Sarah Jane (Mrs.). farmer, Bythen
Churchill Herbert, baker, West street
Churchill Joseph, saddler
Clark Ephraim, Black Dog P.H
Clotworthy John, builder, Fore street
Comner Wm. tailor & draper, South st
Cox Henry, farmer, Heiffers
Cruwys George, farmer, W. Piliven
Cutcliffe Mrs. farmer & landowner, Coombe & New house
Dart William, farm bailiff to Mrs. Cutcliffe, Cannington & Coombe house
Davey John & William, farmers, Malson & Wilson
Dinner William, blacksmith, Fore st
Dummett Thomas, Angel P.H
Eastman James, police constable
Eastmond Edmund, farmer, Muxeries
Fewings Edmund, farmer, Wheadon
Fox Fowler & Co. bankers (branch) (Herbert John Mansfield, manager), wed. & fri. 11 to 2 ; draw on Barclay & Co. Limited, London E C
Gill Hedley Thorne, assistant overseer & clerk to Parish Council, Lakelands
Greenslade James, shopkeeper, Fore st
Greenslade Susan (Mrs.), news agent, Rose cottage
Greenslade Wm. shoe ma. Bow court
Gunn Charles, Hare & Hounds P.H
Gunn Charles, wheelwright
Gunn Ellen (Mrs.), nurse, South st
Harris John, farmer, Foxdon
Hill John, farmer, South Grendon
Hodge Hy. mason & shopkpr. North st
Holcombe Claude & Mary (Misses), dress makers
Holcombe William, tailor, Fore street
Holt George Frederick M.R.C.S.Eng., L.R.C.P.Lond. physician & surgeon, Lawn cottage
Hooper Robert, piano tuner, Fore st
Huxtable James, farm bailiff to Mrs. Cutcliffe, New house
Lee Robert, builder, Ebrington's row
Lee William, farmer, South Coombe
Maire Amos, miller (water) & shopkpr
Maire Harriet (Mrs.), dairy, Mitre ho
Manley Wm. butcher, Gunn hole
Mansfield Herbert Jn. grocer & draper
Matthews Harold, farmer, Nth. Coombe
Maunder Frank, butcher, Fore street
Maunder Lloyd, farmer, East Essebere
Norrish Geo. gardener to Mrs. Cutcliffe
Partridge Charles, farmer, Lakelands
Partridge William, shoe ma. Rosemont
Phillips Ann (Mrs.), nurse, The Square
Pickard Ann (Mrs.), tailoress, West st
Pullen George Henry, jun. draper & grocer, Post office
Roberts Thomas, farmer, Newland
Robins George, farmer, Adworthy
Rowcliffe Isaac, farmer, Penford
Selley George, butcher, South street
Selley John, farmer, Hill town
Shelley Percy Wilfred Graham M.R.C.S., L.R.C.P. physician & surgeon, & medical officer & public vaccinator, No. 6 district, South Molton Union & Cruwys Morchard district, Tiverton union, Cypress ho
Stone Sidney John, resident sergeant, Police station
Stoneman Richard, miller (water), Drayford mill
Thomas Richard, farmer, Leat
Tolley John, farmer, Hellinghayes
Tolley Wm. insur. agent, Rosemont
Trawin Henry Tapp, wool stapler & drug stores
Tucker George (Mrs.), farmer, Wilson
Tucker William Henry, farmer, Higher Queendart
Tucker Wm. Henry, shoe ma. West st
Venner Robert, thatcher, Drayford
Venner Thomas, thatcher, Godswell
Vicary Charles, farmer, Dart Raffe
Volunteer Battalion (4th) Devonshire Regiment (L Co. Capt. Percy W. G. Shelley ; Wm. C. Carter, drill instructor)
Way James, carpenter
Way Mary (Mrs.), dress maker
White Frank, farmer, Fore Down
Whitfield Selina (Mrs.), baker
Witheridge & District (The) Dairy Co. Limited (William Greenslade, sec.), dairymen
Wreford William, farmer, Bradford

Entry for Witheridge in *Kelly's Directory*, 1902

The sketch shows how Witheridge Church looked, probably for centuries, before the ancient wooden spire became so decayed that it was decided to remove it and add in its place a further 40ft to the tower. This was done in 1841, and the Churchwarden's accounts for this and the following year show some of the costs – 'Paid Thomas Western (Mason) towards the Tower £150' – 'Paid John Brawn (Carpenter) his bill £47-17-4' – 'Paid Thomas Western his bill £51-5-6' – 'Paid Mr Barrett for fresh hanging the bells £25-5-0'.

At the left of the picture is the Poor House, where the destitute were given a home. The Church bore the cost: for example in the 1820s and 1830s they paid one shilling a year for 'Sweeping the Poor House Chimneys'. From time to time rethatching was necessary, and in 1821 it cost £3-11-0 to do this, with a further £3-9-0 for 'Reed and Spars'. The Poor House was demolished in the late 1830s to make room for the road widening necessary for the new Turnpike Road from South Molton through Witheridge to Tiverton in 1840.

In 1842 there is an account for '114 Nitches of Reed for the Churchyard wall', and a thatcher's bill for £1-18-6. A length of this wall can still be seen on the right of the churchyard behind Mr and Mrs Payne's property; it is likely that at one time it ran all along between the churchyard and the Vicarage garden.

The sketch shows the gates, gatepillars and railings. As the inscribed stone in the wall beside the gates today has the date 1833 on it the sketch can be dated between 1833 and 1841 when the spire was removed and the tower raised.

From the *South Molton Gazette* of 27th February 1886

## DESTRUCTIVE FIRE AT WITHERIDGE.

On Monday night a disastrous fire occurred at Witheridge. The scene of the conflagration was a block of four houses adjoining the churchyard, three of which are owned and occupied respectively by Mr. Joseph Churchill (saddler), Mr. J. Denner (wheelwright), and Mr. W. Way (carpenter). The fourth belongs to Mr. H. Trawin, who vacated it some weeks since. The whole property had thatched roofs. Fire was discovered shortly after seven in the chimney of the unoccupied house, and before steps could be taken to extinguish it, it had gained a firm hold, and seriously threatened to envelope the whole block. A telegram was dispatched to Tiverton (the nearest town with a fire engine) and the West of England fire brigade, in charge of Mr. John Grater, proceeded to the spot, arriving there shortly before ten. By this time the fire had played great havoc with the buildings, the roof of which had fallen in, and there being very little left on which the firemen could direct their efforts. Moreover there was a scanty supply of water —only sufficient, it was estimated, to enable the engine to play on the flames for ten minutes. Consequently the firemen, after assuring themselves that there was no danger of the fire spreading to other property, deemed their services of no avail and returned home. It should be stated that the destroyed houses were isolated ones. Fortunately Messrs. Churchill, Denner, and Way, were able to remove the bulk of their furniture and movables before the fire had made a substantial headway. All the houses are insured—two in the Royal Farmers' Office, one in the West of England Office, and one in the Caledonian Office. The loss, therefore, is limited to a few things that could not be removed before the buildings were enveloped.

A Witheridge correspondent writes:—On Monday night a fire of an alarming nature broke out in the centre of the town, by which five houses were totally destroyed. Between 6 and 7 p.m. an unaccountable volume of smoke was noticed in the Square. This gradually accumulated till its source was discovered by flames bursting forth from Mr. Trawin's house. Everyone was immediately on the alert, straining every nerve to extinguish the flames. The fire engine was telegraphed for from Tiverton, but arrived too late to render any practical assistance, for by half-past nine the fine block of buildings, which for so many years has graced the Square, was utterly destroyed. The houses were occupied by Messrs. J. Churchill, saddler; Trawin, wool merchant; Denner, wheelwright; and J. Way, glazier. Mr. Denner recently bought his house, so it is doubtful if his effects were insured. The last fire occurred in the village about twelve years ago, when the premises of Messrs. Mansfield and Selley were destroyed.

The premises of Mr J. Churchill are those on the right of the picture: until the mid-1870s they formed the Bell Inn of which Mr Churchill was the Landlord.

To show some of the difficulties faced by the Tiverton Fire Brigade details follow from the description in the *Tiverton Gazette* of 23 June 1914 of a fire at Charnaford Farm, not far from Witheridge. On this occasion the brigade was telegraphed for from Morchard Road Post Office. On receipt of the telegram the Lieutenant was sent for, and on arriving at the Fire Station he discharged the maroon. At this moment one of the horses for drawing the engine was harnessed to a mowing machine in People's Park, while the other three were attached to carts collecting refuse. Within nine minutes, however, of the maroon going off a start was made with the engine, four horses and five men. The journey was an exceedingly trying one for horses owing to the hilly conditions of the country, but the four animals accomplished the ten miles in just over ninety minutes.

HARVEST FESTIVAL.—The Harvest Festival was held on Wednesday. Matins, with a celebration of the Holy Communion, took place at 10.30 a.m., a public tea in the National Schoolroom at 5 p.m., and evensong, with a sermon, at 7 p.m. Both the church and the schoolroom had been profusely decorated with flowers, fruit, cereals, and ferns by various ladies of the parish, and presented a picturesque appearance. The attendance at the tea was very satisfactory, considering the stormy weather. The trays were taken by Miss Benson, Mrs. Gordon, Mrs. Mansfield, Mrs. G. H. Selley, Miss Cutcliffe, the Misses Pullen, and Mrs. R. Way, the proceeds of the tea being devoted to the fund for the improved lighting of the Church. The evening service, which was of a special thanksgiving character, was fully choral. The opening portion and the prayers were given by Rev. J. P. Benson. The first lesson was read by Rev. H. A. Mitchell, and the second lesson by Rev. W. H. Thompson. Rev. Canon Trefusis occupied the pulpit, and drew some good practical lessons from Hosea ii., 21, 22. The collections, both morning and evening, were in aid of the Royal Benevolent Agricultural Institute.

There is no War Memorial here so the date must be before 1919. The name over the shop is Holcombe. The Misses Holcombe ran a dressmaking business together there from the turn of the century until about 1920, then Miss Claude Holcombe continued on her own until the 1930s.

CONGREGATIONAL SUNDAY SCHOOL.—On Sunday the anniversary sermons in connection with this school were preached by the Rev. W. P. Duke, of Ilminster. In the afternoon the children were examined in Scripture knowledge and gave evidence of having been well instructed in the essential truths of the Gospel. On Monday they enjoyed their usual sports, and then marched in procession to the School-room to partake of tea. All adjourned to a public meeting in the chapel, presided over by the Pastor. The financial accounts were satisfactory, and the general attendance for the past year, and the attention of the children to the instruction imparted, were reported by the superintendent to be very good. The number of children on the register is 109. Addresses followed by the Revs. Pope, Duke, Bishop, and Classey.

### Anniversary

Witheridge Congregational Sunday School anniversary was held on Sunday last. Rev. R. W. Carr preached in the morning and presided over the afternoon service at which the young people gave recitations and musical items. At the evening meeting, presided over by Ald. W. Lake, C.C., the young people again took part.

The vicar with the bellringers in 1922 is the Rev. Melrose, who preceded the Rev. J.A.S. Castlehow.

In 1936, £309.10s. was spent on alterations and improvements to the Methodist Chapel. The wall at the back was rebuilt, and the old railings, red brick wall and bushes by the doorway were replaced by a glass-covered porch giving access to the chapel and schoolroom. The reopening, seen here, was attended by, among others, the Chairman of the Exeter District.

In the 1920s the landlord of the Hare and Hounds (pictured here on the left) was Mr William Reed. His wife was very proud of the limeash floor in the pub and used to wash it with scald milk every day to make it shine. The Hare and Hounds was popular with travelling salesmen, such as those from Avon Tyres and the Anglo American Oil Company.

*Tiverton Gazette*, 7 April 1914

### WITHERIDGE SQUARE

Witheridge Parish Council wrote enquiring who were liable to repair Witheridge Square.

Mr. Trawin: I should like to ask the Clerk whether we should be called upon to repair it?—The Clerk: This Council is the authority liable to repair public highways, but a Square is not necessarily a highway repairable by any authority.

Mr. Trawin expressed the opinion that coming from Drayford across the Square it would be main road, also from Mr. Pullen's to the Church. Mr. Adams, a former Highway Surveyor, he added, once coated the entire Square with material.

The Chairman said the Council appeared to be liable.

Mr. Trawin asked whether the Council could prohibit shows and standings being set up in the Square.—The Clerk replied that if it was a highway it should be kept for public use. A highway might be dedicated to the public subject to all sorts of things; there might, for instance, be a footpath across a field subject to a right to plough the field. Possibly Witheridge Square might be subject to all sorts of things; there might, for instance, be a footpath across a field subject to a right to plough the field. Possibly Witheridge Square might be subject to a right for the Lord of the Manor to allow the erection of booths and shows.

Mr. Dymond: Has Witheridge a charter for holding fairs?

The Chairman: I think it has, for two or three fairs. (To Mr. W. S. Gardner, Surveyor): What repairs have you done?—Mr. Gardner: None inside the watercourse, sir.—And you have been Surveyor how many years?—21.

The Chairman: I fancy I have known the road coated.—Mr. Tolley: It was done 23 years ago.—The Chairman: By the rates?—Yes.—Mr. Trawin said that the complaint had relation to damage recently done by a lorry; it was not desired that the whole surface of the Square should be coated, but that ruts which were several inches deep should be filled in.

The Chairman: The Surveyor had better be instructed to do what is necessary.—Mr. Trawin: Would it not be wise to communicate with the Lord of the Manor—he might like to do it himself?

Mr. Gardner: I do not know whether the Council are aware that the police are searching out who is responsible for this property, and try to find out about the tolls.

After further discussion, it was decided to restore the surface where it had been damaged by the traction engine, and to communicate with the Lord of the Manor.

Mr Joe Churchill, saddler, has his name below the upstairs window of the Pound House where he lived. He was also a barber and did a post round. It was not unusal for him to lather a customer's face, shave one side, and nip across to the Angel for a few drinks before coming back to shave the other side.

The Pound House in the Middle Ages was the place or 'pound' where stray beasts were impounded and not released until a fine had been paid. In 1396 on 'Saturday next after the feast of St Nicholas', Witheridge Court fined John Fattecote not only for letting his horse stray and be impounded, but also for breaking into the pound and releasing it.

Mrs Olive Vernon's father, Mr W. Baker, was the blacksmith in Church Street but when in 1907 the tenancy of the Angel was to let, Mrs Baker said, 'We'll go for it', and they got it. They held it until 1937 when it was taken over by their daughter Ruby and her husband Mr Bill Buchanan, who held it for another thirty years. Mrs Vernon was born in the Angel and remembered as a child having to cut up sugar with sugar cutters, trim the 14 lamps and clean their reflectors and lamp globes and fill them with oil, clean off the grease on the candlesticks with soda and water. If the children had any spare time in the autumn they'd 'take an old sack bag down to the marshes at New Bridge for acorns', which they took up to old Mr Amos Maire at Ditchetts where he kept a dairy and a pig.

Many men used to start the day by calling into the Angel at 6 a.m. for a pint or quart of cider. Some heavy drinking was done, and often Mr Baker would 'jump the counter' and try to get fathers to go home to their families once he thought they'd had enough. 'Some of the women round the Drang used to break out and drink, and the pins would come out of their hair and it would draggle down. Some would cross the Square in their flannelette nightdresses to buy drink to take home and drink in bed'.

'Old Sir Ian Amory used to call in after hunting, for bread and jam, and then go up to change leaving mud all up the stairs and on the white vallance around the bed. Once the hounds were put in the coach house and killed all the fowls gone to roost.'

In the 1920s and 30s a canvas tent was set up in the middle of the Square for two or three weeks at a time; it seated 50 people and showed silent films – 'old films that were throw-outs with lines going up and down the screen'. Mrs Vernon's husband Bill used to play the piano for these films.

Mrs Baker was once told by old Mr Pullen that he remembered the original Angel burning in about 1830; it used to be thatched, and the same height as the house next door.

This picture was taken in the 1930s. To the right is the old Police House, with the sign 'Devon Constabulary'. There were two cells, living accommodation for the Sergeant and his family, and rooms for the Constable. The cost of the building was £425 and the builder was John Selley of Witheridge. Particular attention was given to the heating and ventilation systems for the cells; a special stove, which circulated warm air through ducts, was supplied at a cost of £12-10-0. Thus the prisoners had 'central heating' while all the other rooms had fireplaces. The cells, with their original doors, but without the locks and bars still remain.

Mrs Millie Churchill is on her way past the Police House to the Pound House where she and her husband Joe lived. She taught at the church school.

Witheridge did not alter much in the 1880s until just after the 1939-45 War. Then in 1946, following the demolition of Anstey's Court, the first part of Butts Close was built, extended in the 60s and 70s with the widening of the main road to the east, and the building of the school and fire station in the field beyond the white chapel at the top centre of the picture. Fore Street was widened, Ebrington's Row (with its straight line of outhouses at the top left of the picture) was knocked down to make way for Appletree Close. The Parish Hall was opened in 1966, Lakelands and Chapple Road and Greenslade Road developments took place. This is probably the last picture taken before the whole process began. Even the row of cottages between the bakery and the Angel is shown here.

The beginning of 1946 saw the building of Butts Close as reported here in the *Western Times*, 4 January 1946

NEW HOUSES.—Building operations have started on the 24 Council houses which are to be built on a site just above the village.

This is the oldest picture of Fore Street, and must have been taken before 1907, because in that year a fire destroyed much of the row of cottages on the right of the street in the middle distance. It broke out early one morning in the yard of Rogers, the builders. Mr Bill Bragg rode to Tiverton to get the fire brigade, while others ran around the village rousing help and fetching ladders and buckets. But the thatch was well alight, and all they could do was to try to prevent it spreading even further. By the time the fire brigade had galloped out from Tiverton, several houses were gutted. The road was blocked for several days, and carts had to go around by North Street, Ebrington's Row and out by the Manse.

On the right is Anstey's Court (now the garden opposite the garage); one of the occupants was Mr Bert Adams who kept a blacksmiths shop on the triangular piece of ground at the top of the village at Chapner Cross. Those living in Anstey's Court were among the first tenants of the Butts Close houses when they were built after the 1939-45 war.

On the left is Lawn Cottage, occupied at the time by the schoolmaster and schoolmistress of the British School, Mr and Mrs Carter. It was not until the 1920s that it began its career as a garage.

Three scenes in Fore Street in the 1920s and 30s. In the earliest (above) there is no sign of a garage business. In the second (left) there is a pump, and in the close-up of Doble's Garage there is a number of typical advertisements of the day, including Hercules Cycles, and the 'Winged Mercury' head of the National Benzol petrol sign.

These premises were the only ones in Witheridge to suffer damage in the Second World War, and not from enemy action, but from our American allies.

Before the invasion of Europe in 1944 American tank forces used to carry out manoeuvres on Exmoor, and one day a loaded tank transporter came up through the village from South Molton; it already had had a brush with the surroundings, for there were telephone wires draped round its Grant tank. Unfortunately it got wedged where the road narrowed by Greenslade's shop, with its hubs touching the buildings on both sides of the road. The driver revved up and the transporter moved forward taking the corner of the shop with it, and leaving the bed upstairs hanging out over the street. The American comment was, 'What are these goddam houses made of – paper?' The walls were rebuilt, but a few weeks later another transporter arrived and this time most of the village went to watch it knock the shop down for the second time, which it duly did.

There were American troops encamped at Deer Park Cross, Cruwys Morchard, for a time; they patronised the Angel, 'beer in one hand and whisky in the other', and the hedgebanks between Witheridge and Cruwys Morchard were said to be littered with their beer bottles.

Judging by the angle of Mrs Tidball's milk can it is empty, so she is probably on her way to the dairy. With the horse and cart is Mr George Partridge, who worked for Mr Charlie Maire. Mr Maire was the miller at Witheridge Mill, and owned the first traction engine in the village. On the right the Hare and Hounds sign projects out over the street, this inn was certainly in existence in 1850 when Samuel Foxford kept it. The house in the centre, Sunnyside, was occupied by Mr W.H. Rogers, a private schoolmaster. Mr Rogers wrote verse for all kinds of occasions, using the pen name 'Vigilo'. The street lamp on the garden of Sunnyside has a cross piece against which the lamplighter leant his ladder.

Mr and Mrs Bill Welch stand outside their cottage (the only one of three remaining). There is doubt whether West Street was ever called Queen Street. It was only called West Street because the Post Office insisted that it had a name. The cottages opposite Cannington House were cleared to make way for garages. On the left is Fern Cottage and on the right is the corner of the Methodist Chapel, which was opened on 25 June 1859; among the bottom course of stones are many engraved with the names of some of those who contributed to the cost of the building.

The main road through the village between the Square and Trafalgar Square was known as Queen Street. This picture dates from the 1900s. The lady in the apron outside her cottage is Miss Crook. Behind her is a group of men outside the blacksmiths. The cobbles on either side of the road are clean, in contrast to the road itself. On the right is The Mitre; at the time it was a private house, later to be given in the 1930s together with some land (of which the present Parish Hall field formed part) as an endowment for a public hall by the Benson family. The Mitre and most of the land were later sold, and the Parish Hall was built.

*Express & Echo*, 24 April 1936

### HISTORIC BUILDING AS PUBLIC HALL ?

#### Ballot to be Held in Witheridge

Under the instigation of the local British Legion, a parish meeting was held last night at Witheridge to consider the proposed gift by Miss Grace Benson, of Barnstaple, of an historic coaching house, The Mitre, for use as a parish hall. Miss Benson's offer was made following the appointment of a Legion sub-committee to consider building a hall.

A committee has now been formed through the efforts of the Rector (Rev. J. A. S. Castlehow), the British Legion chairman, and Mr. R. N. Culhene (hon. sec.) to go into the cost of converting the premises for public use, and of maintenance.

It has been decided to hold a ballot of the whole parish as to the need for a hall.

*Western Morning News*, 24 April 1936

### HISTORIC BUILDING FOR PUBLIC

#### Witheridge To Decide By Ballot

#### GIFT TO PARISH

Witheridge residents la.. night met to consider further the proposed gift by Miss Grace Benson, of Barnstaple, of an historic coaching house, known as The Mitre, and situated in the centre of the town, for use as a parish hall.

Recently the local British Legion formed a sub-committee to consider building a hall. Mr. Benson offered the use of The Mitre, and the British Legion decided to call a meeting to include all the parish interests.

##### CONVERSION COST.

Through the instrumentality of the rector, Rev. J. A. S. Castlehow, the chairman of the British Legion, and Mr. R. N. Culhene, hon. secretary, a committee has been formed to consider with Mr. Benson the estimated cost of converting the premises into various halls to be used by the Legion, Women's Institute, and other parochial organizations, and the estimated cost of upkeep afterwards.

The committee have decided to hold a ballot of the whole parish to vote as to whether they require the hall or not.

Miss Benson has been closely associated with Witheridge for many years, and has befriended the parish on many occasions. Her brother, Preb. J. P. Benson, is a former vicar of Witheridge.

There is a horse-drawn seed-drill outside the blacksmith's, and a set of drags (harrows) leaning up against the yard wall of the Angel, on which are posters advertising livestock and property sales.

Mr and Mrs Kingdom in the garden of Littlebourne.

There has been a bakery on this site for over two hundred years. In the 1780s Mr William Burgess set up a bakery business here on this spot, which is occupied by Reed & Son today. It passed to Mr Henry Burgess, who on his death in 1855, left it to his daughter Elizabeth. She sold it to Mr William Whitfield, in whose family it remained for over eighty years, until it was bought in 1943 by Mr William Churchill. His father had started a rival bakery at the bottom of West Street in the 1880s. Mr Churchill closed his own business on buying Whitfields. Mr Raymond Reed, Mr Churchill's nephew, started to work for him in 1943, and bought the business in 1955. Mr Reed's son Paul also works there. The old faggot oven was replaced in 1943 by a coke-fired system, which in turn gave way to oil in 1970 and then to electricity in 1984. For the faggot oven the baker would buy a hedge or coppice wood, have it cut and then have a woodrick made of it close to the road, so that cartloads could be collected as needed. Bakers not only baked their own goods but allowed customers to bring their own cakes and also their Christmas and Sunday dinners, to be baked in the oven; it was not unknown for a husband to fail to recognize his own family's dinner when he came to collect it, and to go home with the wrong one.

*Middle right*

In about 1900 Mr Amos Maire stands outside his premises (now Ditchetts), with his second wife Harriet and his son William; he was also the miller at Witheridge Mill.

*Bottom right*

Ditchett's, just across the road from the bakery, became a shop in about 1926, when Mr Jim Buckingham (seen here on the left) started the business. He sold sweets (including 'chews' at twelve for a penny), biscuits, cigarettes, and greengroceries from the productive garden at the back. The terrier in the doorway is 'Nip', who was given to Mr Buckingham's son Arthur on leaving school by his schoolmaster, Mr Andrews. The date is about 1933. The shop closed in 1950.

Mr Lionel Gunn, Mrs Gunn and Miss Joyce Gunn stand in front of their shop (formerly Pullen's, then Culhene's and now the Village Stores) in the 1920s.

The advertisement states that Pullen's was established in 1825. In the Directory for 1850 Mr Henry Pullen is described as, 'grocer, draper, druggist, stamp distributor and agent to the Norwich Union Insurance Company'. In 1870 Mr G.H. Pullen appears as grocer, draper, provision dealer and bootmaker, while Mr Henry Pullen retained an insurance agency, this time for the Royal Farmers Insurance Co. By 1893 Mr G.H. Pullen has become a 'private resident' and is living at Rosemont, while Mr G.H. Pullen junior is entered as 'grocer', to which he soon added 'draper and Post Office'. Not long ago the original glass doors with the name 'Pullen' engraved on them formed the entrance to the shop now called 'The Village Stores'. The name of the Pullens is however still retained in Pullens Row.

POST OFFICE HOUSE,
WITHERIDGE, Jan 1889
E. Worlington Clothing Club

**Bought of G. H. PULLEN,**
**Draper, Grocer, & General Warehouseman.**

MOURNING GOODS, &c.

A LARGE ASSORTMENT OF BOOTS & SHOES ALWAYS IN STOCK.

5 Club Tickets 10/4 £2 11 8

PULLEN'S
CHOICE
BLENDED TEAS
PURE. FRAGRANT. EXQUISITE FLAVOUR.

FRESH-GROUND
COFFEES.
ESTABLISHED
1825.

# G. H. PULLEN,
## DRAPER,
### Grocer & General Warehouseman,
POST OFFICE, WITHERIDGE.

AGENT FOR THE ALLIANCE ASSURANCE Co.

## REVISED POSTAL SERVICES

### IMPORTANT CHANGES IN THE WITHERIDGE AND RACKENFORD DISTRICTS

On and from Wednesday, May 1st, a considerable rearrangement of the postal services will take place in the Witheridge, Rackenford and Nomansland areas. The changes have been made in order to provide for day mail services in these districts.

The first delivery will be earlier than at present and in some of the outlying districts there will be an acceleration of two or three hours. An afternoon delivery at Witheridge and a delivery to callers at Nomansland and Rackenford have been provided for. A morning collection will be made from all boxes in the area in conjunction with the first delivery, and correspondence for neighbouring towns will obtain delivery the same day.

A notice of the alteration in Postal address has been delivered to the occupier of every house concerned, and in order that the full advantage of the revised services may be derived it is desired to emphasise the necessity for the use of the new postal address on and after the 1st May, 1935. Failure to comply with this request is likely to cause serious delay in transmission of letters and inconvenience to correspondents.

The names of the places affected are: Bradfords (Witheridge), Creacombe (Rackenford), Nomansland, Rackenford and Witheridge. After May 1st the postal address of these places will be Tiverton, Devon instead of Crediton as heretofore.

It may be of interest to know that it will now be possible to post a letter or parcel in Tiverton as late as 3 p.m. for delivery in the town of Witheridge or to callers at Nomansland and Rackenford.

The revised services will involve the employment of extra motor drivers and the vehicle employed will cover an annual mileage of approximately 50,000 miles.

*Opposite page:*
On the right stands Mr George Selley, who took over the butcher's business at Cannington House in the 1880s. Beside him is his first wife who had had five children by the time of her death at the age of twenty-four in 1891. Mr Selley married again and his second wife also bore five children. The slaughterer is Mr Ernest Hill, and on the left is Mr Wreford of Bradford.

*South Molton Gazette*, 27 February 1892.

### WITHERIDGE.

THE WEATHER.—A Witheridge correspondent, writing on Saturday, said :— On Friday the snow fell very heavily here during the whole of the day with a strong north-east wind, causing very large drifts in the roads so that vehicular travelling was stopped. The mail cart was able to come yesterday but unable to go out again in the evening. The rural postmen were unable to go their rounds. The carriers from Exeter took their vans laden with goods as far as possible and left them at a farm near the road and then took home their horses. It is to be hoped that men will soon be put on so as to clear the roads, that traffic may again resume its usual course. The thunder on Saturday morning seems to have cleared the atmosphere and we are glad to see the sun making its appearance again although a little more snow has fallen. I hope that both frost and snow will soon bid us adieu for this season.

*Tiverton Gazette*, 5 January 1907.

Mr. C. Baker, the Witheridge mail cart driver, met with an accident a few days ago on his return journey from Morchard Road station in the early morning. On turning a corner the horse shied, pitching Mr. Baker in the road, and the horse and vehicle on one side. Luckily Mr. Fred Leach was close behind with another horse and trap; in a short time the horse was got up, and Mr. Baker was taken to the doctor at Morchard Bishop, where it was found that he had received a very severe cut across the forehead, which had to be sewn up, the doctor inserting four stitches.

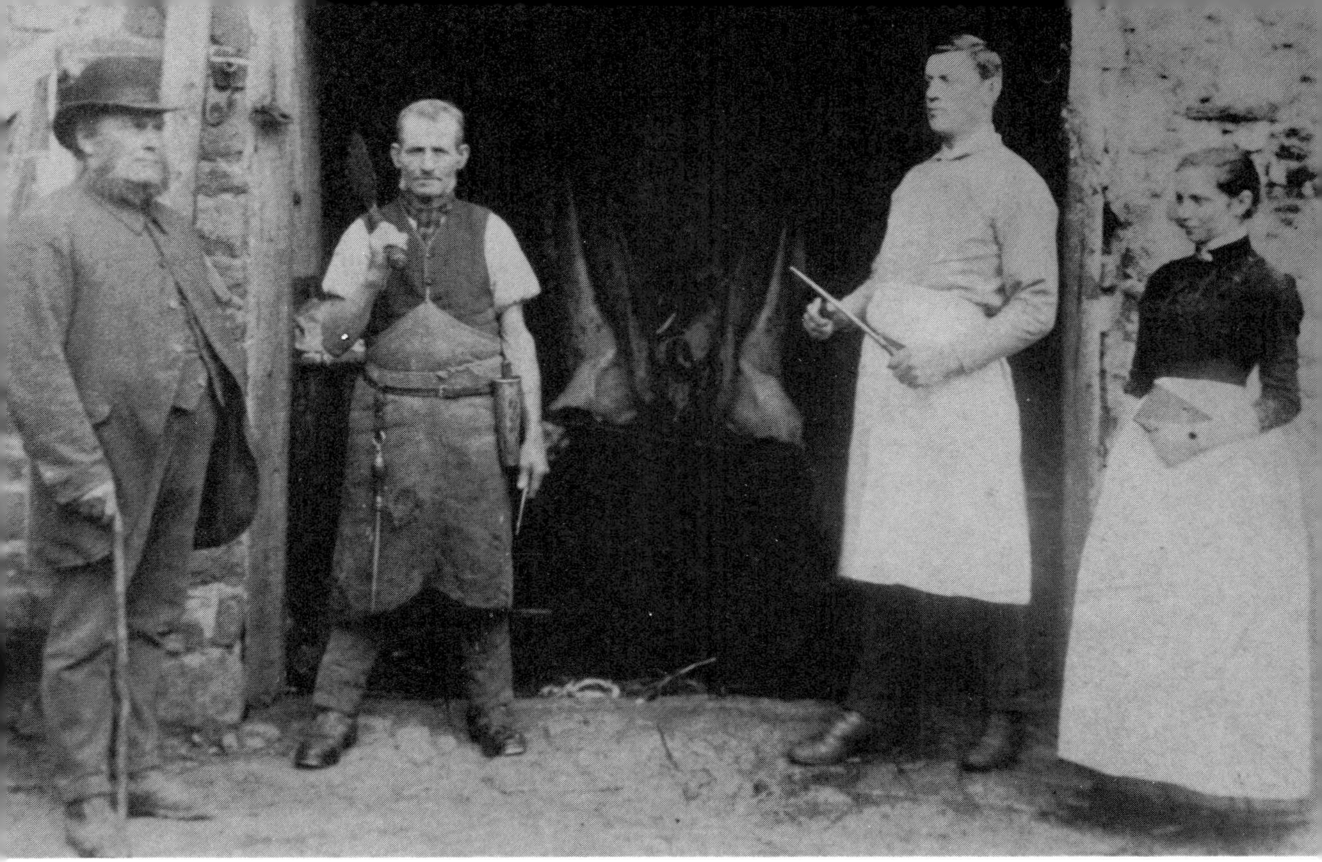

Mr Lloyd Maunder was born at Essebeare Farm in 1874, and began his business around the year 1900. He bought his first pony and trap (seen here driven by Mr Fred Leach) and began wholesale and retail dealing in butter, poultry and eggs. The picture was taken in the roadway outside The Firs (the fir trees have not been growing long); in the background is Gordon House and Anstey's Court. The vehicle has carriage lamps, a long brake lever working on the offside rear wheel, and double elliptic springs front and rear. The butter was elevenpence halfpenny (5p) a pound.

From these humble beginnings the firm now employs over 500 people and has a huge turnover. Had the railway come to Witheridge as planned, then this development might have been in Witheridge.

Fore Street, Witheridge, 1891

Mr

Bot. of F. J. P. MAUNDER & Co.

FAMILY BUTCHERS.

F.J.P. Maunder & Co. were the family butchers in Fore Street

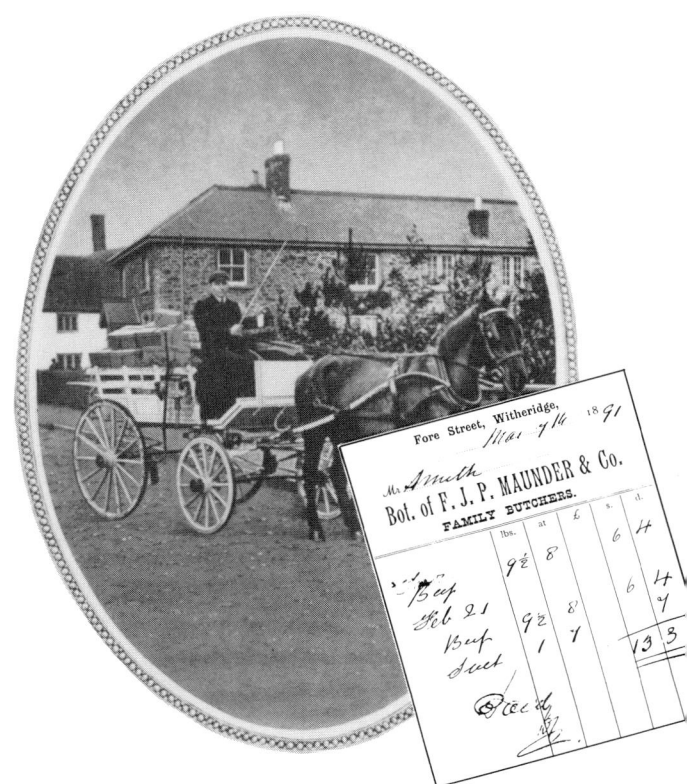

Mr Edward Elworthy was certainly in business from 1857 to 1893, although not until about 1870 did he add 'Chemist' to 'Veterinary Surgeon' in his description. Among the items listed on the account are 2lbs Lamp Black, Linseed Oil, Condition Powders, 5 packets Farmers Friend, Aromatic Vinegar, 1 gallon Harness Oil and a Lamb Teat.

Report of the Directors of the Witheridge and District Dairy Company Ltd, in 1896.

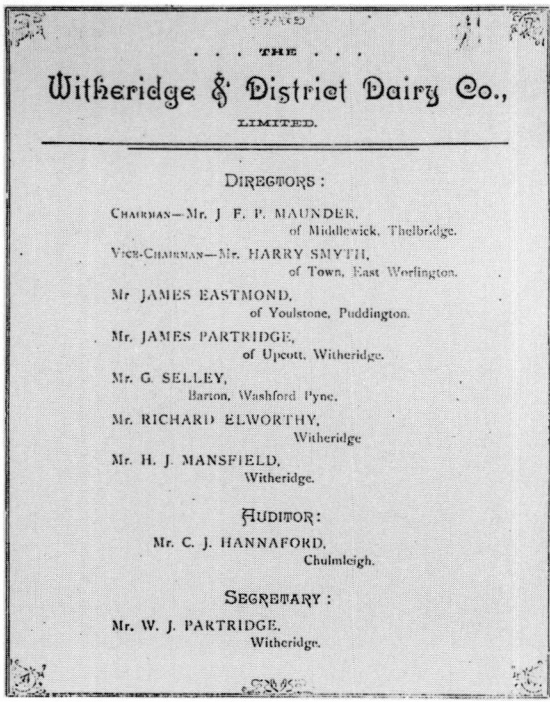

**Witheridge and District Dairy Co., Ltd.**

NOTICE is hereby given that the 2nd Annual Meeting of the Shareholders of this Company will be held at the Factory on Monday, the 24th day of February, at 6 p.m., to receive the Report of the Directors, together with Statement of Accounts to the 31st January, 1896; to declare a dividend; to elect Directors for the coming year; and to appoint an Auditor.

By order of the Board,

**W. J. PARTRIDGE,**
Secretary.

*Witheridge, 12th Feb. 1896.*

Black Dog was, 'a rough cider pub, with a low ceiling inside and as dark as a dungeon. Each round was a two-quart jug of cider per man.' The inside consisted mainly of a big kitchen with several settles. The beer and cider were drawn out at the back. The last landlord, Mr Ephraim Clark, allowed 'roadsters' (as tramps were called) to spend the night in the attic, but made sure they handed over their cigarettes and matches before going up, for fear of fire. The pub closed around the end of the 1914-18 war, failing to get its licence renewed owing to objections by the police that there were 'too many bolt-holes to watch'.

Also in the Square there were the Angel and Commercial (now 15 West Street), and up the road by Trafalgar Square was the Hare and Hounds. The Commercial housed the horse-drawn mailcart which took the post to Morchard Road Station; the mailcart was a 'square red box and the driver sat on top to drive the horse'. It is said that on one occasion the bells of a local church were stolen and thrown in the river, and two detectives came and stayed at the Commercial, going out each day 'to do their detecting disguised as navvies with red handkerchiefs round their necks'.

Up until 1914, Witheridge Band played in the Square on Saturdays in the Summer, with their beer or cider on the ground beside them. Not that the ground was all that clean then, for most people who lived around the Square kept fowls, and let them out in the mornings to scratch in the Square or the churchyard. It was 'fowls everywhere', 'but they all knew their way home'. They also knew their way to other people's property, for the fowls from the Angel used to make their way up the road to old Miss Crook's cottage opposite the Mitre and scratch in the wooden boxes of flowers by her door, and she used to throw her stick at them.

Printed by William Pollard,
40, North Street, Exeter.

Transfer License granted at Special Sessions.

At a Special Sessions holden at *the Town Hall South Molton.*
on the *Thirteenth* — day of *July* — 18*83* for
the Division of *South Molton* — in the County of Devon.

**COUNTY OF DEVON,
to wit.**

We, being *three* of Her Majesty's Justices of the Peace, acting in and for the said Division, and being the majority of those at the said Sessions assembled, hereby, pursuant to Section 4 of The Intoxicating Liquor Licensing Act, 1828, and the Acts amending the same, License one *Ellen Gunn* of *Witheridge*

in the same County, and transfer to h*er* the License now ~~held by~~ *lately held by her late deceased husband William Gunn* of *Witheridge aforesaid* — a Licensed Victualler, ~~or a Beer House Keeper, Coffee House Keeper, Eating House Keeper, Confectioner, Licensed Dealer in Spirits, Refreshment House Keeper, Wholesale Spirit Dealer, the holder of a Strong Beer License, Dealer in Liquors and Sweets~~, and granted on the *third* — day of *September* last, authorizing h*im* to hold an Excise License to sell by retail at a House ~~and Shop~~ situate at *the Town and* *and known by the sign of the Black Dog Inn* in the Parish of *Witheridge* in the said County of Devon, for Intoxicating Liquor, ~~Beer, Cider, Wines, Spirits, Liqueurs, and Sweets~~, to be consumed *either on or off* the Premises, in pursuance of the Statutes 6 Geo. IV. cap. 81 ; 11 Geo. IV. & 1 Wm. IV. cap. 64 ; 11 & 12 Vict., cap. 121 ; 23 Vict., cap. 27, sec. 3, 7, & 8 ; 23 & 24 Vict., cap. 114 ; 24 & 25 Vict., cap. 21, sec. 3 ; and Acts amending the same.

And we hereby authorize the said *Ellen Gunn* —
to apply for and hold the said Excise Licenses so held by the said

This transfer to be in force from this day until the Tenth day of October, 18*85*.

Witness our hands

*Bawden*
*Geo Sutcliffe*
*W. T. Fairleigh*

Note.—Fill up the particulars of License
as in the Original License.

The Black Dog

The date is about 1917, and Mr and Mrs Baker, Licensees of the Angel, are at the entrance with their daughters Hetty, Olive, Cora, Stella and Ruby. Their sons William and Leslie are away on War Service.

*Tiverton Gazette*, 7 February 1939.

# FORMER WITHERIDGE LICENSEE

## DEATH OF MR. W. BAKER

The death occurred on Tuesday of Mr. Wm. Baker, who for 30 years was landlord of the Angel Hotel, Witheridge. Three years ago he retired and went to live at Exmouth. In Witheridge he took keen interest in parochial affairs, and was a member of the Parish Council. He leaves two sons and four daughters.

The funeral was at Witheridge on Friday afternoon when the Vicar of Witheridge (the Rev. J. A. S. Castlehow) officiated. Interment was preceded by a short service in the Parish Church.

Immediate mourners were: the widow; Messrs. W. and L. Baker, sons; Mrs. J. Gay, Mrs. W. Vernon, Mrs. W. Buchanan and Miss S. Baker, daughters; Messrs. Alfred, Bert and R. Baker, brothers; Messrs. J. Gay, W. Buchanan and W. Vernon, sons-in-law; Mrs. W. Baker and Mrs. L. Baker, daughters-in-law; Mrs. A. Baker, Mrs. Albert Baker and Mrs. R. Baker, sisters-in-law; Mr. Leslie Baker, nephew; and Mr. Kennard (Exeter).

Bearers were Messrs. W. Southwood, F. Leach, C. Maire, W. Gold, R. Rodd and J. Churchill.

The public sympathisers included the Preb. Rev. P. Benson and Miss Benson, Messrs. C. Maire, W. Lake (Worlington), F. Hall, H. Chapple (Rose Ash), E. Osborne (Worlington), J. Mills, R. N. Culhene, W. J. Woolacott, W. Cox, B. Adams, F. Tidball, R. Tarr, S. Way, S. Hayes, W. Kingdom, T. Smyth, S. Selley, J. Adams, T. Bucknell, P. Fewings, G. Selley, F. Criddle, W. Southwood, J. Stone, G. Shapland, F. Venner, J. Bradford (Black Dog), F. J. Tarr, W. Vicary, E. Turner, W. E. Turner, H. Holman (Exeter), E. Cole, A. Nott, J. Knight, E. Hutchings, W. J. Cole, J. Vicary, W. Alford, H. Greenslade, W. Reed, S. C. Ward, S. Elston, Rowcliffe, J. M. Adams, S. Cole (Worlington), C. Thorne, A. Tucker, Mrs. Whitefield, Mrs. Hutchings, Mrs. R. Rodd, Mrs. H. Churchill, Mrs. W. Gibbs, Mrs. W. Pyne, Mrs. Knight, Mrs. W. Gold, Mrs. Bourne, Mrs. W. Darch, Mrs. Elston (Denhay), Mrs. Palfreyman, Mrs. Williams, Mrs. W. Churchill, Mrs. E. G. Palmer, Mrs. S. Selley, Mrs. Hooper, Mrs. F. Criddle, Mrs. Horridge, Mrs. J. Crang, Mrs. S. Brent, Mr. and Mrs. W. Hill, Mr. and Mrs. F. K. Maunder, Mr. and Mrs. W. Chapple, Mr. and Mrs. G. Shapland, Mr. and Mrs. F. Horridge, Mr. and Mrs. R. H. Burrow, Misses P. Adams, G. and M. Burrows (Worlington), V. Manley, M. Davies and S. Nott.

There were many beautiful floral tributes.

*Tiverton Gazette*, 30 November 1901.

Whether it is advisable for the Tiverton Fire Brigade and steam fire engine to attend every country fire to which they are summoned is a question which requires careful consideration. On Tuesday the firemen received a call to quell an out break at Witheridge, and started off with promptitude. But when they arrived on the scene they found that the conflagration had subsided.

Considering how long and hilly is the journey to Witheridge, it would have been as well, when the fire was got under, to have despatched a messenger to warn the Brigade that their services were not required. Men who are willing to sacrifice their time and energies in the public good are entitled to every consideration. In addition to this it must be remembered that the wear and tear in connection with a costly fire engine are considerable.

A fact which cannot be too strongly emphasised was brought to light in connection with a second fire the following evening. Though the outbreak, which took the extraordinary form of a blaze in a mangold heap, occurred quite close to the town—on Poolanthony Farm—some time elapsed before a hydrant could be found. Blundell's School brigade were ignorant of any hydrant within 700 feet of the seat of the fire : as a matter of fact there was one within 350 feet.

I am assured that steps are now being taken to make every hydrant conspicuous. After applications extending over six months, Mr. Norman has obtained a renewal of a promise that plug-plates shall be put to all hydrants on the School premises. Hydrants, however, are useless without water. Last Wednesday, when at length a hydrant was discovered, there was no water in the main ! Had the outbreak happened at one of the boarding houses the result might have been disastrous. I am told that Blundell's has two supplies, but they are seldom both on. One is a mere squirt : the other from Warnicombe, is better, but on less often.

In one respect the Heathcoat Fire Brigade, who were called to the Poolanthony fire nearly an hour after the Tiverton Brigade, showed the borough firemen the way. When they arrived on the scene their steam was already up, whereas the Tiverton engine was not even then ready for action. A question as to the length of time it took the Tiverton Brigade to get up steam, elicited the statement that they had not brought their "specially prepared fuel." But if not, why not ?

That the Blundell's Fire Brigade is one which may be relied on to do good service, if required, was convincingly proved on Wednesday. The smartness with which they turned out would have done credit to a much better equipped Brigade, and had there been any water in the main they would have made it unnecessary for the Tiverton steamer to get to work. That they should have attained to such a degree of efficiency is little short of marvellous, when one considers the many changes which of necessity occur in the personnel of the Brigade. To Mr. G. H. Norman, who takes a great interest in the Brigade, much of the success is due.

After the Tracey Green fire in 1945 there was a strong demand for a local fire service, and in 1946 the Witheridge Fire Brigade was formed as part of the then National Fire Service. They are seen here as a group at the entrance to the old fire station (formerly the bus company garage) in North Street, and lined up in front of their engine (a converted post office telephone van) and tender. Those standing in the group are, from the left, Mr W. Somerwell, Mr W. Lewis, Mr W. Clements, Mr R. Priest, Mr S. Selley, Mr L. Baker, Mr R. Tapp, and Mr W. Osborne. Seated are Mr F. Kingdom, Mr F. Leach, Mr W. Vernon, Sgt Palmer and Mr J. Luxton.

**Rackenford Fire**

Witheridge fire brigade were called at 1.30 a.m. on Saturday to a fire at Lower Thorne Farm, Rackenford, where the farmhouse was practically burnt out.

*Western Times*, 4 June 1948.

*Tiverton Gazette*, 30 November 1901.

### WITHERIDGE SANITATION.

Dr. Body, Medical Officer of Health, made a detailed statement of the presence of scarlet fever at Witheridge; and also as to a nuisance arising from the drainage there, which was very offensive and decidedly injurious to health. Complaint was also made as to the foulness of the water supply after heavy rain, attributable to the neglect of the caretaker. After some discussion, in which the local Councillors took part, it was decided to give the caretaker notice to determine his engagement, to serve a notice on the managers of the National Schools to abate the nuisance complained of, and compel them to carry their drains in another direction.—The Committee appointed to consider the East Worlington water supply was requested to visit Witheridge and inspect the other nuisances complained of, and report thereon.—It was also decided to prosecute in one case, where a notifiable disease had not been reported on.

*Tiverton Gazette*, 6 June 1939.

A circular letter has been sent to Witheridge householders by the Clerk to Southmolton Rural District Council, stating that he had been directed by the Council " to advert to the present temporary shortage of the water supply at Witheridge and to request you to arrange for your household to exercise economy in the use of water. A scheme for a new water supply for Witheridge is in course of preparation, and will shortly be submitted to the Ministry of Health. In the meantime further immediate steps are being taken to augment the supply to remedy the present shortage."

In a letter to the Minister of Health, enclosing a copy of the circular, Mr. R. N. Culhene states that the representatives of the 94 families who signed the recent petition wished to inform the Minister that no point raised, although astounding, was exaggerated.

Despite an improvement there were, with the exception of about 20 houses, whose tap level was the lowest in the village, houses that were getting no water. Water was turned on at about 8 o'clock in the morning, and from 10.30 there was no water except at those low points.

*Tiverton Gazette*, 13 June 1939.

# WITHERIDGE WATER SHORTAGE

## SOUTHMOLTON R.D.C.'s SECRET SESSION

## NO STATEMENT ISSUED

Shortage of water at Witheridge, already the subject of a petition and a letter from residents to the Minister of Health, was discussed by Southmolton R.D.C. on Thursday, but a report by the Sanitary Inspector and the subsequent discussion was taken in committee. No reason was given for this decision, and no statement indicating what steps the Council intend to take was issued to the Press.

*Tiverton Gazette*, 23 May 1939.

Signatures to the following petition are being sought in Witheridge in view of the serious water shortage. The petition will be submitted to the Ministry of Health.

The petition asks the Minister to instigate an immediate investigation, and proceeds:

" After a very wet winter, one week of dry weather brought about a serious shortage, so that some houses were, and still are, without water altogether, and with insufficient water to flush any lavatory."

" If an epidemic did break out, very serious consequences would follow. In the event of a fire there would be no possible chance of abating it.

" Hundreds of pounds have already been spent on a scheme which is known to admit surface water. Another scheme to cost £4,000 has been approved, which we are sure will not be successful on maintaining a supply through a normal summer.

Rogers' builders yard in Fore Street (now Stoneman's) was rebuilt after the big fire in 1907. Mr Rogers is on the left, with Mr Ford and Mr Hutchings

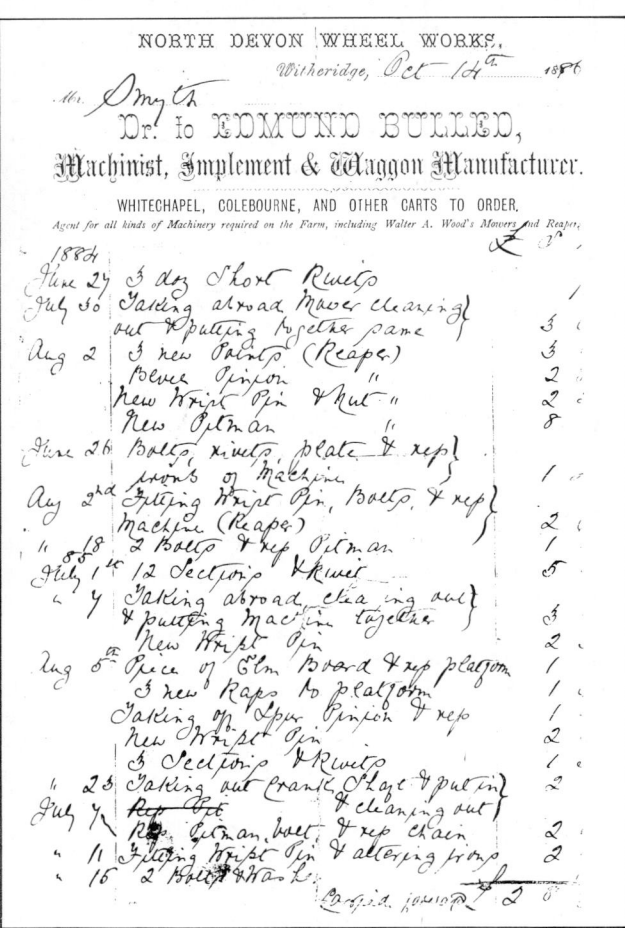

Edmund Bulled, wheelwright.

Mr Bill Gold followed Mr Edmund Bulled as wheelwright. He stands here on the left with Mr Jack Bristow on the right and Mr Victor Stenner between them. The business was carried on in buildings to the right of the present Wheelwright Cottage. The date is in the 1930s.

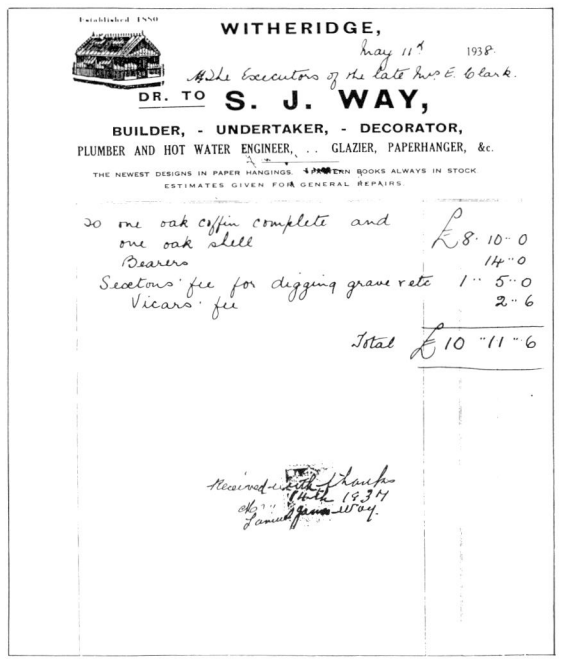

To one oak coffin complete and
one oak shell      £8. 10. 0
Bearers      14. 0
Sexton's fee for digging grave rate   1. 5. 0
Vicars' fee      2. 6

Total   £10. 11. 6

Received with thanks
*March 1934*
*Samuel John Way.*

S.J. Way, undertaker

John Baker was an established blacksmith and agricultural implement maker by the year 1870. He was succeeded firstly by Charles Baker, and then by William Baker who for many years combined the job with that of helping his wife run The Angel.

*South Molton Gazette,* 17 September 1887

Venner, thatcher

This is Bradford Mill in the 1920s, or possibly earlier. Mr W. Roberts was the last miller there; it ceased working in the 1930s.

Bradford Pond was a popular venue for walks, either along the path past Witheridge Mill, or down from North Street along the path to Yeo Woods, and then past East Yeo. A few people used to drive out in a pony and trap and walk in from the road with their picnic. It is remembered as a beautiful lake covered in water lilies.

*1885*        Mr Smyth          £   ,   d

            To Jane Phillips

      For Grinding from Nov 17th

      To May 7

      33 Bushels wheat at 5d pr B     13   7

*Do*     185 Do Barley at 2d pr Do     1   6   3

      148 Do crack corn at 2d pr Do     1   4   6

                         £ 3   4   6

      20 Bushels Wheat @ 4/6.     4   0   0

      Paid May 25 85.            3   4   8

        Thomas Stoneman.         7   5   4

For the last half of the nineteenth century, Drayford Mill was in the hands of the Phillips family, but by 1902 Mr Richard Stoneman was the miller, and continued to be so until it closed in the 1940s.

Donne's map of Devon of 1765 shows watermills in Witheridge Parish only at Bradford and Drayford. It does however show a Witheridge windmill on the high ground near Millbarn Cross, an area that was once one of the outlying parts of the Parish. Other outliers were Yeatheridge and Little Witheridge; all three were allocated to other parishes when the boundaries were tidied up in 1885. The Ordnance Survey Map of 1809 does show Witheridge Mill by the Little Dart. It ceased operation in the early 1950s. The course of the old mill leat can still be seen, together with the remains of the weir.

During the 1914-18 war, the roads around Witheridge were so badly damaged that it was said that two men setting out down Coombe Road from Witheridge in separate ruts would not see each other until they reached Drayford. Rather than repair the roads, and create good access for a new tar plant, Notts preferred to establish a depot on the main road above New Bridge. One of the photographs shows part of the machinery. The various grades of stone reached the depot by means of an aerial ropeway from Coombe Quarry on trestles over the valley of the Little Dart. The wire ropes were continuous and the buckets which were clipped to them, had small wheels for running on the small rails at the quarry end where the shute operator had to be very quick to get them filled as they passed. The hours of work were 7 am to 5 pm, Monday to Friday and to 1 pm on Saturday. The rate of pay was ninepence halfpenny an hour, and if work had to stop because of the weather, then the men had to stay at their place of work without pay. In the 1920s it was all hand-drilling, one man turning the drill and one man striking, until Holman's of Camborne brought out a steam drill driven by a traction engine. This was later replaced by the compressed air drill. At the quarry face, two men worked together at loading a skip, and then pushed it down to a crusher; the rate of work was about 8 tons per hour. The quarry foreman in the 1920s was Mr Bill Welch, who had a habit of taking a lift in one of the buckets from the quarry to the depot, until the day when someone with a grudge or a sense of humour waited until he was halfway along and then knocked the ropeway out of gear and left him stranded above the river in his bucket.

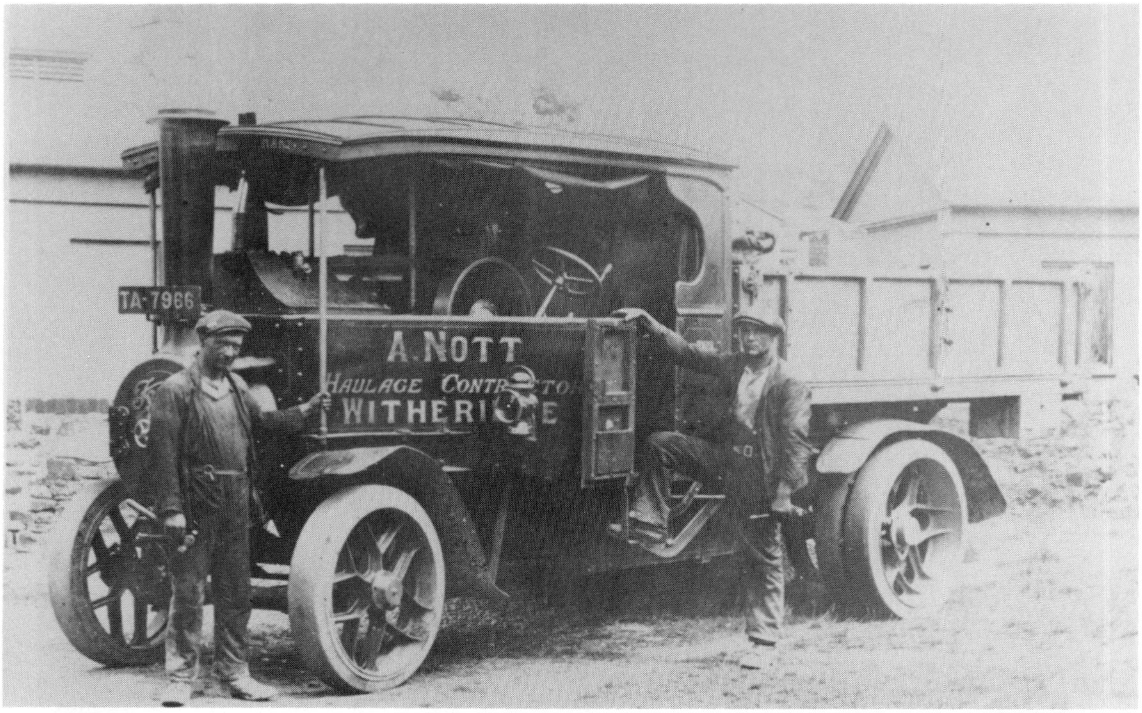
TA 7966
A. NOTT

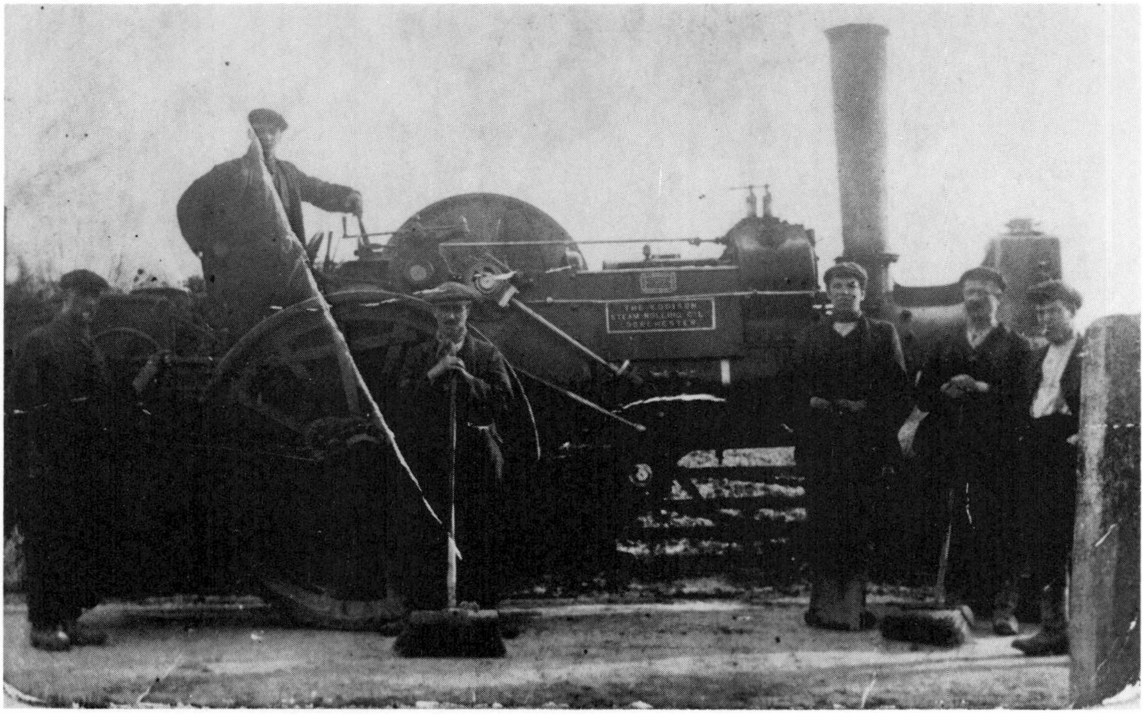

COMBE QUARRY WITH...

The bill is dated 1884-5 and is for work done by Mr John Tidball, whose wife has receipted it at the bottom. The writing is none too clear, but it can be seen that the cost of bringing a parcel from Exeter varied from 2d. to 4d., no doubt depending on size and weight. 'Carriage of geese' was 7d. and 'carriage of rabbits', 4d. 'Three jars from Tiverton' cost 6d. to bring to Mr Smyth of Town, East Worlington. The brake is outside High Cross, Trafalgar Square, where the Tidballs lived: on the box of the brake is Mr Tom Tidball, with his wife in black behind him. At the horse's head is Mr Fred Tidball.

Witheridge from Coombe Road

Before 1920, Witheridge relied on carriers for the transport of goods and people, and the two local carriers were Thomas's and Tidball's. When this photograph was taken (early 1900s) Thomas's were running services to Tiverton on Tuesdays, Thursdays and Saturdays, and to Exeter on Fridays. Tidball's offered Tiverton on Tuesdays, Exeter on Thursdays and South Molton on Saturdays. Here is young Bill Thomas (with the reins) and his brother Ernest, on their way down to Coombe House with the laundry basket to collect the Cutliffe's laundry. They will also be picking up baskets at Witheridge and Cruwys Morchard vicarages for delivery to Tiverton. Bill Thomas started driving at the age of 11 when his father Mr Mark Thomas died in 1902. With his brother for company, he thought nothing of driving to Tiverton in the winter, doing his errands, getting caught in a snow storm and having to go off and find help and two extra horses to get up Morchard Woods. On another occasion he stopped at Nomansland to collect a passenger, who didn't see him or thought him beneath her dignity, and called out; 'Where's the Boss then?' 'Jump up Missus', said Bill, 'I'm the boss.' 'You'll do, boy', said the lady.

Mr Arthur Bryant started work with Tidball's in 1916 at the age of 13. They drove into Exeter on a Thursday with the trap and carriers van and passengers and village produce for delivery around Exeter. They stayed at the Crown & Sceptre by the Iron Bridge, and returned on Friday, usually having to double up the horses to get each vehicle up the steep slopes at Sandford and Tridley Foot.

Carriers not only provided everyday transport for goods and people, but they were also used as vehicles for special occasions. Here in about 1900 is Mr Mark Thomas on the box of a smart carriage pulled by two greys, a vehicle to be hired for weddings, or to take a group to a party. Mr Bill Thomas often remarked what cold work it was to drive in winter, particularly in snow. Behind the coach is a brake used for outings. Mrs Emily Williams remembered that this was always used for choir outings, when it took them to Lapford Station to catch the train to Exeter and on to Exmouth. It had no cover, but 'the summer was always fine and we never needed a cardigan in those days'. Choir discipline was strict under the Reverend Benson; youngsters had to become probationers and to attend regularly at practise, but until a place became vacant and they could move into a proper choir seat, they did not qualify for the annual outing.

The horses were stabled behind what is now 10 West Street, which in the 1920s, was to become Mr and Mrs Williams' chemist shop. The vehicles were kept next to Trafalgar House.

Not all children walked to school in the old days. Those whose parents could afford it made use of the school conveyance provided by the School Attendance Board for children who lived some distance away from Witheridge. The following excerpt is from the *Tiverton Gazette*, 22 December 1908; 'A special meeting of the School Attendance Committee for Witheridge district was held on Monday to consider the appointment of another person to convey about twenty children from Creacombe to Witheridge Schools. The person has to supply his own van and horse, and the distance covered is about 5 or 6 miles each way. There were twenty tenders sent in, ranging from four shillings and sixpence a day to five shillings and ninepence a day. The tender of Mr Partridge, Willhayes, Creacombe, at 4/6 was accepted, subject to approval. This is one shilling a day less than the last driver received.'

Others who got the job in other years included 'Down the higgler' (or 'heggler' or 'eggler') who delivered eggs, butter and rabbits during the day before taking the children home in the afternoon; and Mr Davey who is shown in the drawing. The drawing has been made from a faded photograph by Mrs Jenny Bidgood.

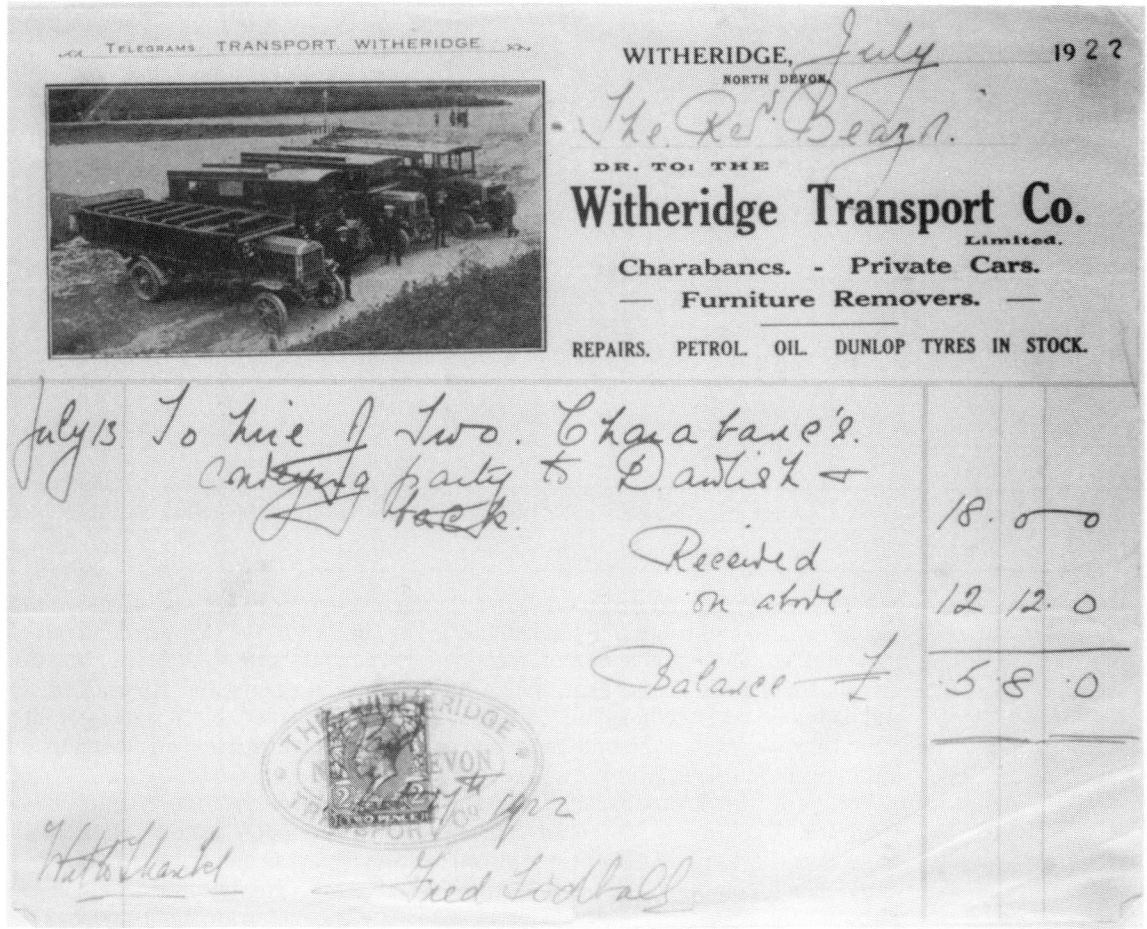

The two carriers, Thomas's and Tidballs', amalgamated in 1921 to form the Witheridge Transport Company, and to celebrate the event they had their fleet of vehicles photographed (they used the picture on their letterheads). Thomas's had bought their first motor bus in October 1915, and the photograph, taken outside a railway station shows it on one of its early outings. The four vehicles are the 'Scout', 'Karrier', 'Dennis' and 'Foden'. The open charabanc-type 'Karrier' was so high off the ground that a ladder was carried to assist the passengers to get in and out. The folding hood was rarely used, but when it was the rows of passengers had to pass it forward over their heads like a caterpillar.

With solid tyres and bad roads it was often a rough ride. On one occasion the 'Scout' was so badly jolted that a baby on its mother's lap was thrown clean out of the window. The baby landed on the grass verge and came to no harm, but the driver stopped the bus so sharply that he was thrown against the steering wheel and had to be taken to hospital. Carbide lights were provided, but if water got into them they went out and 'someone stood on the running board and struck matches if they wanted to see where they were'.

Routes in the 1920s included Tiverton and South Molton direct, Exeter via Sandford, Exeter via Morchard Bishop, Tiverton via Rackenford, and South Molton via Rackenford. There were rival firms in Tiverton and South Molton, but 'they didn't come to Witheridge, they didn't dare'. No hiring was done on Sundays, but once a mistake was made; a booking was taken for the 'Karrier' for a party of people from Stoodleigh on a Sunday and the driver was so worried that 'he slunk all the way there by the back roads so as not to be seen'.

Mr Arthur Bryant learned to drive the Leyland 'Scout' in the 1920s, and recalled that the company's cattle lorry was made by jacking up the charabanc, placing four barrels under the body, unbolting it and driving off. In the 'Scout' the passenger seats were 'only hooked on' and were easy to lift out so as to form a furniture van. Once Mr Bryant and Mr Tidball drove two buses to Exeter with passengers, unhooked the seats, returned to Witheridge, carried out a furniture removal to Newton St Cyres, went on to Exeter, replaced the seats and brought the passengers back to Witheridge.

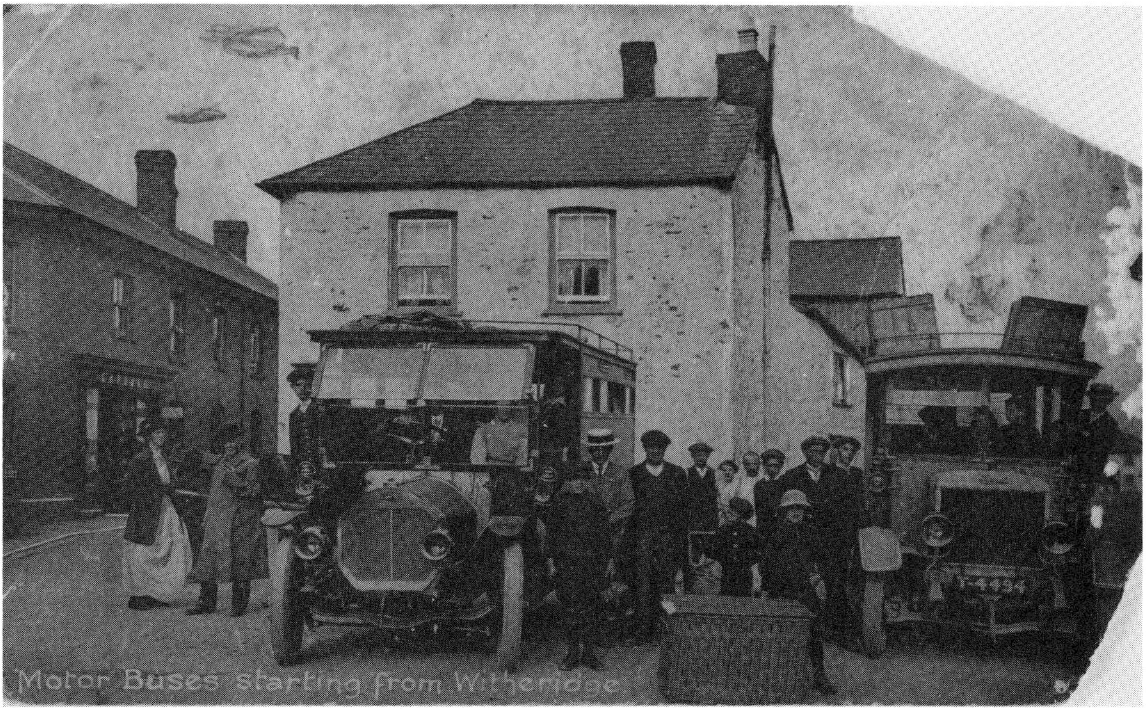

Motor Buses starting from Witheridge

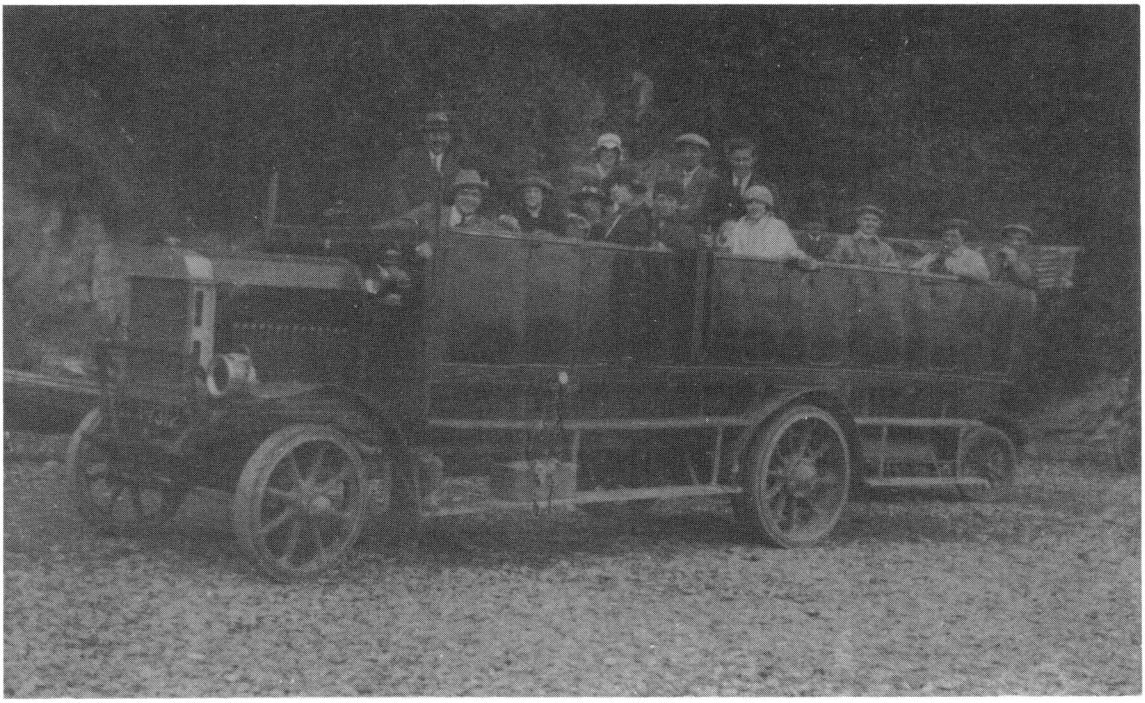

Parties conveyed to all parts

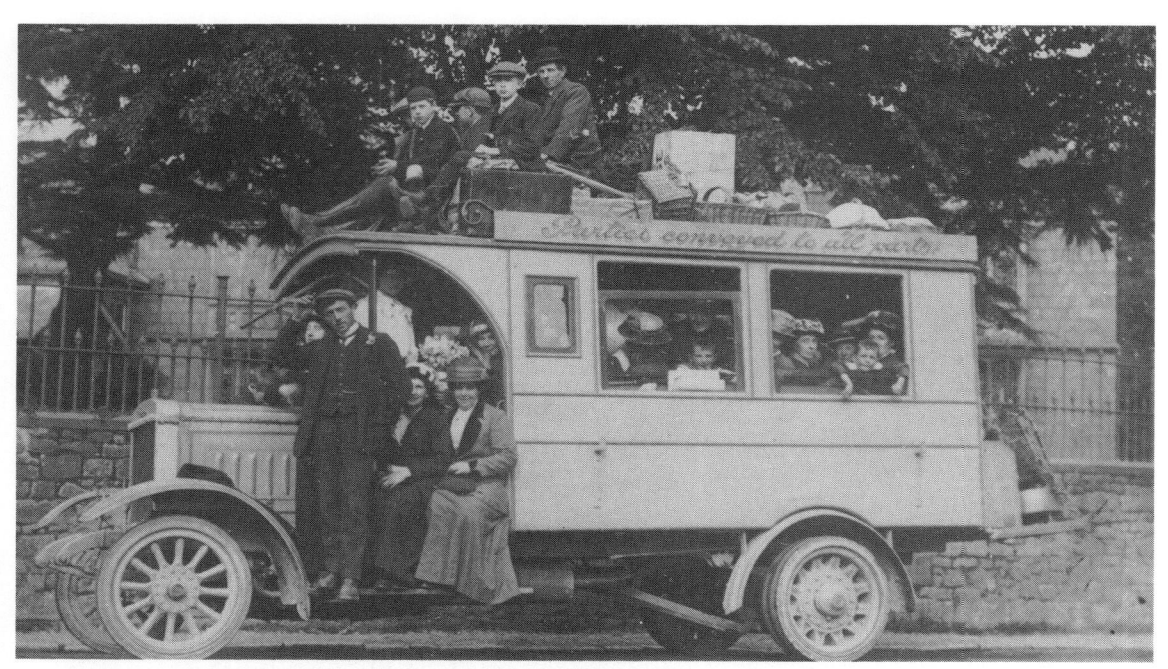

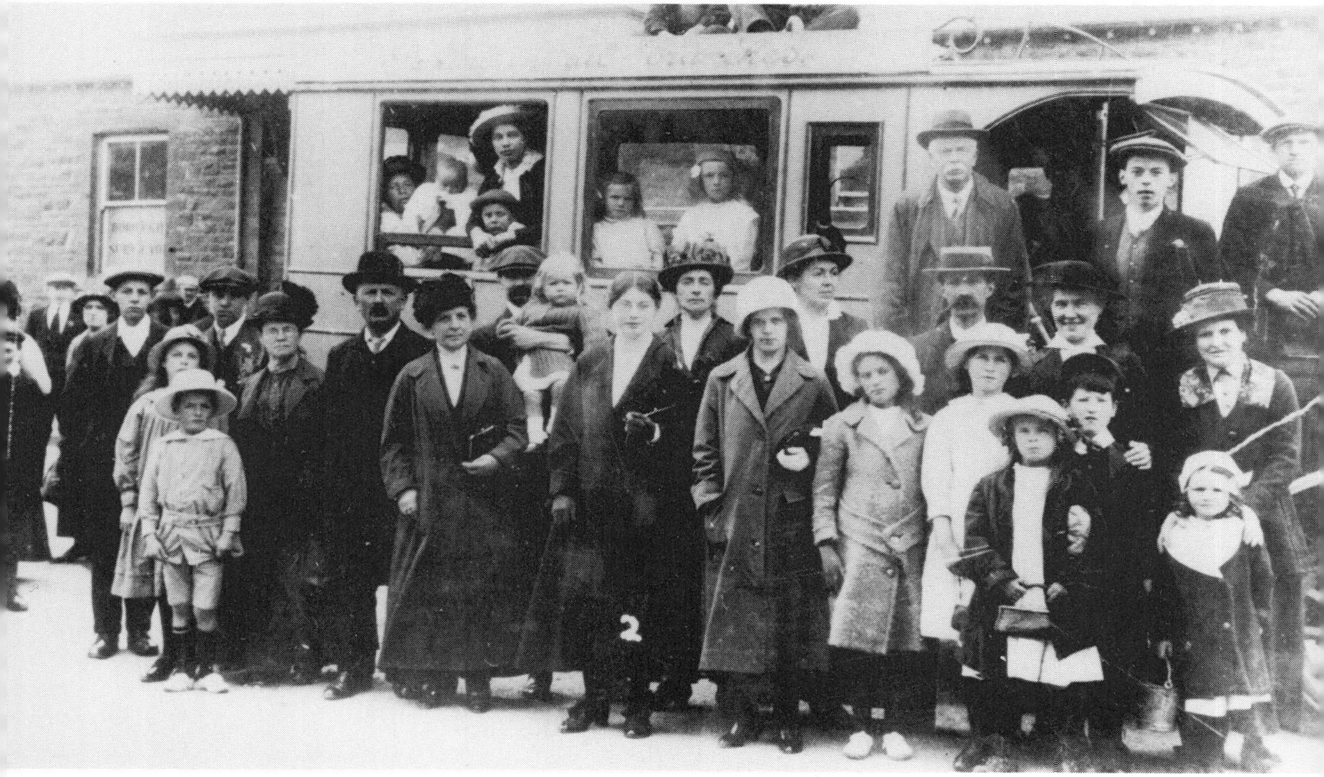

Outings had always been popular, being seen as very special occasions, and interest increased in the 1920s and 30s with the coming of motor transport. The photograph on page 49 with the vicar and the number of children suggests a Sunday School outing. The vicar is the Rev. J.A.S. Castlehow, who was vicar of Witheridge from 1925-65. He was a leading figure in the Tennis Club and the Scouts, and his scholarly work on the history of the Domesday farms in the parish of Witheridge is invaluable.

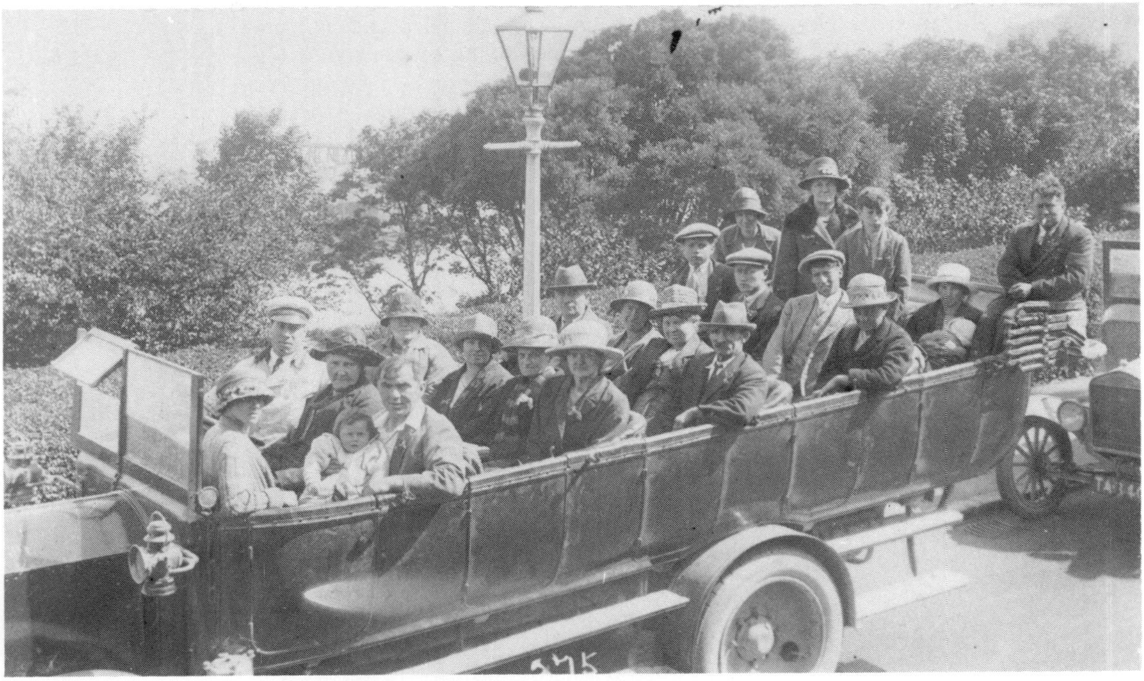

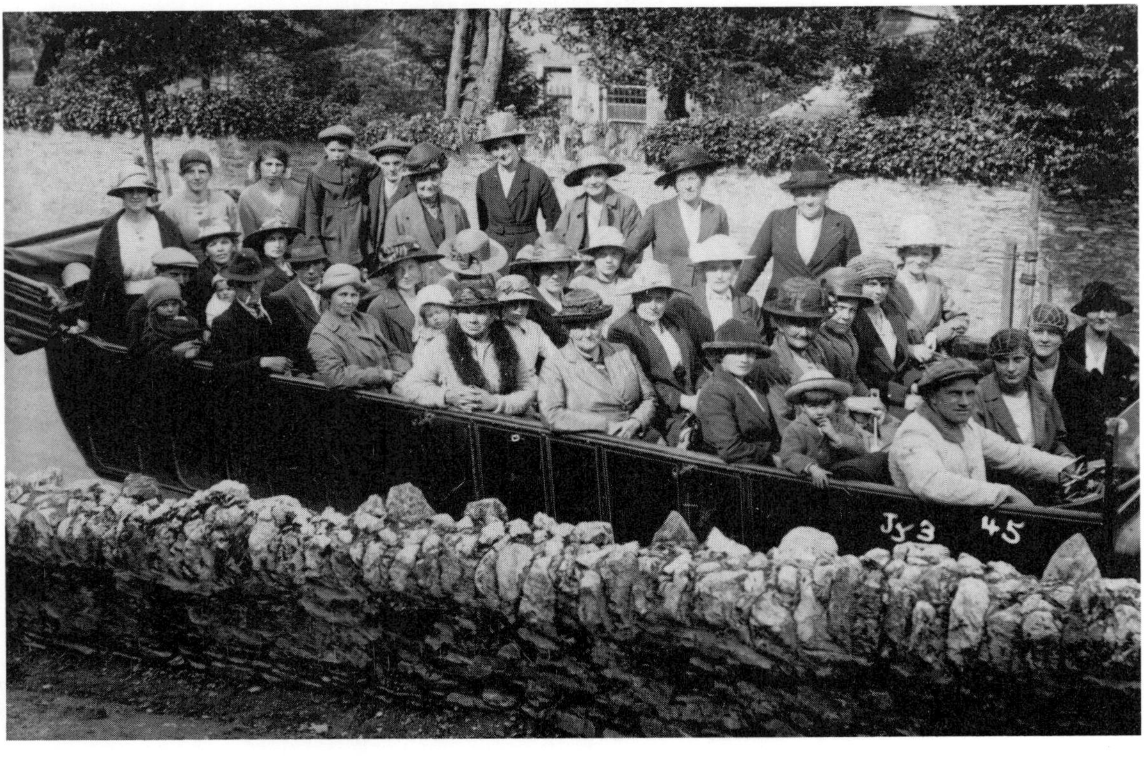
Jy 3 45

Germolene
The Witheridge Transport Co.
52
JY3
LABEL
PAN YAN
BASS & Co PALE ALE

Mrs Emily Selley, second wife of Mr George Selley, has with her in the trap her four stepsons. The date is about 1895.

The Cole family have their picture taken outside the front door of Essebeare in 1897. From the left are Abraham, Courtney, Ellen, Irene, Gwen, Audrey and Bernard.

It is 1917, and Mr William Baker's model T Ford is parked outside the Angel, of which he was the landlord. He has obviously purchased it second-hand, as it is a 1913 model of 23 HP, with wooden-spoked wheels. Miss Cora Baker is standing inside the car, Miss Stella Baker is on the running board, and Mrs Baker and Miss Olive Baker are at the upstairs window.

The two pictures of cyclists in the Square in 1915 show Miss Elsie Blackford with Miss Emmie Pugsley, and Miss Lily Blackford.

Mr W.H.S. Vernon is on his Royal Enfield motorcycle (registration No. TT 1326) in the Angel yard. On the left is the first petrol pump to be installed in the village; cars had to draw into the yard to fill up.

Mr Joe Churchill's Model P Triumph motorcycle and sidecar stands in the Angel yard. On the machine is Mrs Ruby Buchanan, in the sidecar is Miss Stella Baker with young Allan Vernon on her lap. Winston Maunder is on the pony.

This is the outfit of which the following tale is told: One day Mr Churchill's wife Millie said it was time he got it repainted. He was not keen on this, and so he persuaded a friend, Mr Nobby Clark, to do the job. This he did, painting over the dirt and leaving what few bristles there were on the brush stuck in the paint. Not content with this, and being a bit of a joker (as was Joe himself) Nobby then got the Angel shovel and filled the sidecar up with stable manure, beating it down hard before putting the cover back on. Joe eventually came out of the back of the Angel, got on, and rode round to the front door of the Pound House where he lived to take his wife for a ride. Neither his nor his wife's comments when he undid the sidecar cover are recorded!

Mr Joe Churchill, shown here by his 1934 Hillman 10, was the son of Mr Herbert Churchill, the baker, and grandson of 'Old Joe' Churchill. He and his wife Millie lived in the Pound House in the Square. He was a man of many skills – postman, barber, saddler, mason, munitions worker, lamplighter, church clock winder – it was said, 'He would turn his hand to anything'. He was the subject of many tales, of which here is a sample.

Once in the 1920s Joe took a red 'Vote Labour' poster from the Angel and stuck it on Mr and Mrs Vernon's front door. During the night they took it down, wrote 'Chair to be taken by His Worship the Mayor, Joe Churchill', and put it on Joe's door. In the morning they watched as Joe opened his door, looked out, reached back for his bottle, had a swig, put the bottle back, shut the door and went off, not seeing the notice until he returned home. When he did he refused to take it down, saying, 'The b... can stay there'. On another occasion a group went over to Meshaw in a butcher's van with a crate of beer to sing at a concert. Joe had had trouble learning the words of his solo song, so Mr and Mrs Vernon typed out a set of completely nonsensical verses, which they handed to him at the last minute. Joe sang straight through it without batting an eyelid, left the stage, went out to the van and started on the beer. The audience were puzzled by the song and thought it silly. But Joe got his own back; when the concert was over they found there was no beer left!

Joe used to take home a bottle of cider each night, to give himself a good start in the morning. One night he got some fish and chips, and took a bottle over to the Angel for vinegar. As he came out the police stopped him as they thought he'd been drinking after hours and didn't believe it was vinegar, so Joe unstopped the bottle and stuck it under their noses.

One day during the 1939-45 War, the Home Guard arranged a practice spy-hunt in the village, and Joe was up in 'Cox's attic' in Mill Cottages watching out. He saw a stranger walking round the old Police Station and threw Mr Cox's seed potatoes at him, shouting, 'There y'are, ye'r dead, ye b...'.

He is shown here wearing 'plus-fours', which were so baggy that they were referred to as his 'apple-picking breeches'.

Several remembered him as 'a lovely character and so good-tempered'.

The 1915 Dairy Class

This photograph of a cheese-making class dates from about 1916, and was taken in the garden of Rosemont. On the right in the hat and tippet is Miss Laura Whitfield, and on the left is Mr William Henry Rogers ('Vigilo').

This 1931 Dairy School group includes Miss L. Stoneman, Miss C. Selley, Miss O. Hill, Miss R. Selley, Miss E. Ayre, Miss S. Selley, Miss E. Cox, Miss C. Blackford and Miss C. Burridge.

The National School (Church School) was built for 100 children in 1846 at a cost of £400 in place of the old school which had been given to the parish by Richard Melhuish in 1804. He also gave an endowment that brought in enough to pay £14 to the master for teaching 40 poor children to read, and £7 to be laid out in books for the scholars. The school was enlarged in 1898 at a cost of £284. Mr and Mrs Andrews were master and mistress in the first quarter of the century. At this time, some 'went ragged to school', and those who walked in from a distance got soaked in the rain and had to stand by the stove and dry off. Mrs Emily Williams remembered that, 'Mr Carter up at the Chapel School used to use the stick a lot, but Mr Andrews down here had a different manner'. However, sometimes members of the Benson family taught at the National School and brought with them, 'a great ash stick from Bradford' (Bradford Tracey, where they lived). Mrs Burgess went to the National School in 1895 at the age of 5, and recalled being well taught by Mr Andrews who, 'used to cane only a bit'.

*South Molton Gazette*, 5 June 1887.

### WITHERIDGE,

NATIONAL SCHOOL.—On Monday last there was on view at the National School, a tasteful display of needlework, which had been done by children of the different standards. The samples included a variety of useful articles of wearing apparel; and the neat way in which they were finished must have afforded very much pleasure to interested visitors, while at the same time it indicated the great amount of attention and trouble which must have been taken by Mrs. Cornish to bring her pupils to a state of proficiency.

Mr Augustus Andrews was schoolmaster, and Mrs Catherine Andrews was schoolmistress at the National School. The pictures are dated 1920.

Devon County Education Committee.

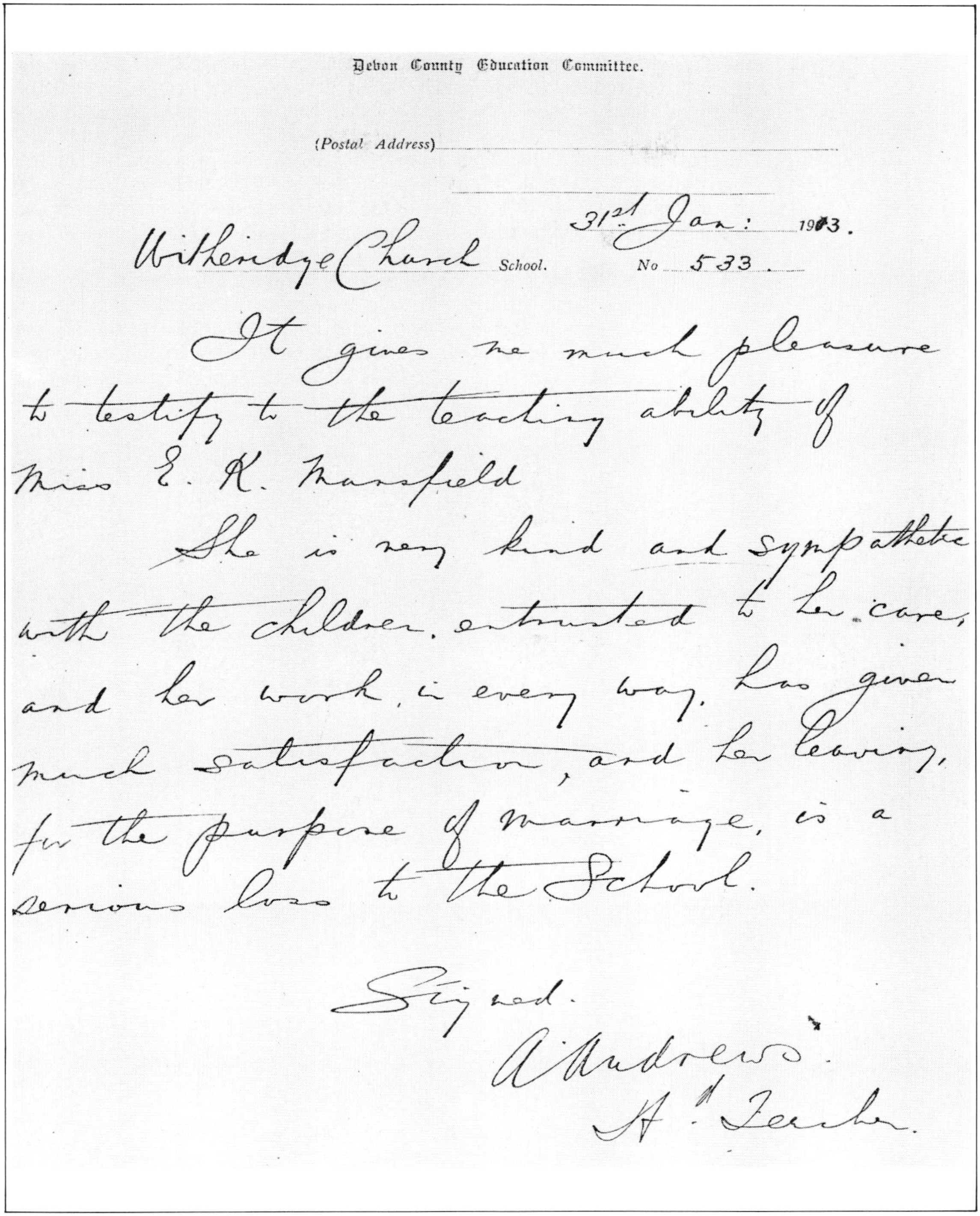

(Postal Address)

Witheridge Church School. 31st Jan: 1913.

No 533.

It gives me much pleasure to testify to the teaching ability of Miss E. K. Mansfield

She is very kind and sympathetic with the children entrusted to her care, and her work in every way has given much satisfaction, and her leaving, for the purpose of marriage, is a serious loss to the School.

Signed.

A Andrews.

Hd. Teacher.

Church School reference.

The British School (Chapel School) was built in 1845 by subscription and was quoted in directories in about 1900 as being for 167 children. Mr Jack Knight remembered Mr Carter (white hair and moustache in the pictures) as being bad tempered. At times he beat pupils so hard that their parents immediately transferred them to the National School. Mr Knight remembered going for a smoke in the Chapel yard in the laurels with half a dozen others; they smoked so hard that the smoke came up from the bushes and was spotted by the Congregational Minister in the Manse, but they were too quick for him. Some children came to school with a penny to feed on for the day: a penny bought two 'halfpenny busters' (currant buns), or four plain 'chudleys' (plain buns about two inches across).

There was much rivalry between the two schools and battles used to take place halfway between them. At Election time they wore party colours to school, mostly Liberal yellow at the top school, and Conservative blue at the bottom. Feelings ran high at Elections, and Mrs Williams recalled her mother refusing to allow children with yellow favours to pass along the front of Ebrington's Row where she lived, as she was a staunch Conservative.

These pupils of the British School in the 1930s pose with their teacher Miss Cora Parr.

An announcement in the *Tiverton Gazette* on 23 June 1908 stated; 'It is proposed to have a sheep-shearing class in connection with the Technical Education Committee in Mr Selley's yard. Mr W. Manley has been appointed instructor'. A week later the following news item appeared in the *Tiverton Gazette*;

It is proposed to have a sheep shearing class in connection with the Technical Education Committee in Mr. Selley's yard. Mr. W. Manley has been appointed instructor.

## WITHERIDGE

In connection with the sheep-shearing classes lately held in Witheridge under the auspices of the Devon County Council, competitions were held on Tuesday in a field kindly lent by Mr. Selley. The judges were Mr. Dart, of Cannington, and Mr. Hooper, of Summer, whose awards were as follows: Class A (under 18 years of age)—1, R. Vicary; 2, H. Selby (Westway); 3, C. Kingdom; 4, J. Davey; 5, G. Greenslade; 6, C. Crook; 7, H. Ayre. Class B (under 25 years of age)—1, T. Ayre; 2, A. Vicary; 3, F. Vicary; 4, H. Flew; 5, G. Chapple; 6, F. Selley. The sheep were sent for the competitions by Mr. F. J. P. Maunder, C.C. After the shearing the competitors and others adjourned to the Angel Assembly room. Amongst those present were Mr. Carter and Mr. Mansfield (who distributed the prizes), Messrs. W. Maunder, F. K. Maunder, G. H. Selley, Andrews, Hooper, Dart, C. Gunn, Vicary, A. Maire, Crook, Hill, and W. Manley (instructor). Congratulations were given by Mr. Mansfield and Mr. Carter to the local Committee for the efficient manner in which they had done the work entrusted to them by the Technical Education Committee of the County Council, and the hope was expressed that another year more classes would be held. Thanks were accorded the instructor.

*Tiverton Gazette*, 30 June 1908.

The photograph shows some of the competitors at work.

*South Molton Gazette*, 11 June 1887.

*Tiverton Gazette*, 9 September 1901.

A CONFIDING TOM-TIT.—At Bythen Farm, in Witheridge, a tomtit, thinking the farmer, Mr. Adams, to be a kind-hearted man, has taken the liberty of building its nest in the letter-box erected in the lane. There she has laid her eggs whilst the letters have been daily dropped on her back, and there she has sat whilst the owner has unlocked the box, taken the letters from off her back, and again locked her up in her secure little nest. Now she may be seen with her little brood peeping from underneath the envelopes with their mouths wide open as much as to say "Thank you for my lodgings, and as you cannot make a very high price of your corn you may as well supply us with our food too."—*Western Times.*

WITHERIDGE.—The crops in this district are nearly all saved in good condition, but in most cases the yield will be very light. The hay crop, I should say, is the worst on record; some was not worth cutting. Wheat will not average 20 bushels per acre, and straw is very short. Early sown oats are a fair crop, but generally speaking the yield is very poor, owing to the cold dry spring. Barley, not much tilled and a very light crop. Roots are looking very promising, especially mangold. Apples are almost a failure. The pasture fields are very bare for the want of rain.—F. J. MAUNDER.

## WITHERIDGE

A number of leading agriculturists of the district visited West Yeo Farm on Monday to inspect the new 7½ h.p. oil engine recently erected by Messrs. Stenner and Gunn, of Tiverton. It is fitted to the thresher, mill, chaffcutter, and pulper, and the various operations were performed in a most satisfactory manner. The party were entertained to luncheon and tea by Mr. G. Cock. Mr. H. Smyth, Worlington, proposed a vote of thanks to the host and hostess.

*Tiverton Gazette*, 5 January 1907.

Mr Isaac Rowcliffe is standing on his cart leaning on his stick, with a group of visitors, and his son Mr Price Rowcliffe is at the horse's head. Mr Rowcliffe farmed at North Grendon, just over the parish boundary in Rose Ash, and then came to live at Penford in the early 1900s.

Mr E. Partridge's family moved to Lower Park in 1908, and with one break of four years he lived and farmed there until his retirement. He went to the British School in Witheridge from 1906 to 1915, and is seen here doing some unpaid Saturday work at Darte Raffe with his younger brother. The daffodils that brighten the road verge above Lower Park grow from bulbs sent over 50 years ago by Mr Partridge's brother from the Scilly Isles.

Cattle graze beside the footbridge over the stream known as Hole Water just before it joins the Little Dart near the old weir. The trees to the right conceal the buildings of East Yeo, now in ruins. To the left are the trees of Yeo Woods, through which the line of the Witheridge Mill leat is still visible today.

It is the summer of 1941 and Mr Bob Woollacott is cutting hay in the field known as Higher Summerlears on West Yeo. He has one of the first tractors in the parish, a Ford on spade lugs, and the first Massey Harris six-foot reciprocating-knife mower.

The three-horse binder is at work at Coombe in 1930.

Harvesting at Coombe in 1934.

The two-horse hay-sweep is at work in the 1920s at Darte Raffe, with Charlie Middleton on the rick and Mr Ned Partridge in control of the sweep and about to mount the seat. The hay is not being pitched to the rick but is being hoisted up by means of a haypole hoist and grab. The hoist was pulled up by a horse and released by the man on the rick.

On 3 June 1935 the farmhouse at Darte Raffe burned down. It was one of the oldest houses in the Parish.

OUS SCHOOLBOYS examining the ruins yesterday of the 13th century farm house on Dart Roffe Farm, Witheridge, which w gutted by fire. It was formerly a monastery. —"Western Morning News" Photo.

*Western Morning News*, 5 June 1935.

*Tiverton Gazette, 11 June 1935.*

# WITHERIDGE FARM GUTTED

## 700 YEAR OLD BUILDING DESTROYED

### VALUABLE CEILING BURNT

A serious fire broke out on Monday, June 3rd, at Dart Raffe Farm, Witheridge, in the occupation of Mr. A. Tucker. The outbreak was discovered about 7 a.m. by Mrs. Tucker and is thought to have originated in the chimney of a bedroom in the West wing of the farm. The fire quickly gained a hold on the thatched roof, and despite the efforts of a willing band of helpers was soon out of control.

At 8.27 a.m. the Southmolton Fire Brigade received a call and proceeded at once to Dart Raffe, under Foreman B. Kingdon. A supply of water was found in a pond in the farmyard, but it was found impossible to check the flames on the roof. Fortunately the whole of the furniture was saved.

The pond was soon pumped dry and an alternative supply was obtained from the Little Dart. Meanwhile the outbreak had spread to the dairy and granary and it was obvious that there was little hope of preventing the farm house from being gutted.

#### 700 Years Old.

Dart Raffe is one of the oldest buildings in the neighbourhood and its age is estimated at about 700 years. A valuable oak ceiling which has been valued at £700 has completely been destroyed.

P.S. Palmer (Witheridge) and P.C. Potter (Black Dog) and Sergeant (Meshaw) were soon on the scene and rendered valuable assistance. Help was also given by Messrs. Chas., Fred and John Leach, William Hutchings, jun., F. Mills, Hunt and employees at Dart Raffe.

Shortly after 10 o'clock the thatched roof began to collapse and by mid-day there only remained the burnt out shell of the farmhouse and the granary. Fortunately the Brigade were able to prevent the flames from spreading to a number of outbuildings which adjoin the farm.

Southmolton Fire Brigade remained at Dart Raffe until late in the evening and finally returned to Southmolton at 11 p.m. They left a relief squad of firemen in charge and together with Mr. and Mrs. Tucker the relief men had an arduous task working all night with buckets of water damping down the still smouldering interior. The firemen remained at Dart Raffe until 9 a.m., when they returned to Southmolton.

*Tiverton Gazette, 7 March 1939.*

# WITHERIDGE FARMERS' UNION

## SATISFACTION EXPRESSED AT ANNUAL MEETING

At the annual meeting of Witheridge Farmers' Union on Monday, 27th ult., there were signs of optimism and satisfaction was expressed at the appointment of Sir Reginald Dorman Smith, as Minister of Agriculture.

Mr. W. B. Hallett, of Lympstone, newly-appointed vice-chairman of Devon county branch, said the Government had obviously taken a serious view of the agricultural situation, and had appointed a new minister. Sir Reginald Dorman Smith had been president of the N.F.U. for two years, and was the man for the job. His appointment had already borne fruit.

Continuing, Mr. Hallett spoke of the fact that in future wheat growers would have the same subsidy as that on barley and oats, as splendid news. Last year had been most unsatisfactory, due to a certain extent, to the unseasonable weather. Farmers' Union figures showed that wheat prices were down by 34 per cent., wool by 46 per cent., potatoes by 27 per cent., fat sheep 23 per cent., compared with 1937. The greatest increase in price was for fruit, which rose by 36 per cent., milk was up 6 per cent., and butter 3 per cent.

Mr. E. Cole was re-elected chairman and Mr. W. Lake secretary. Mr. T. Ayre was elected vice-chairman and appointed representative on the County Executive Committee.

*Crediton & North Devon Chronicle*, 9 November 1907.

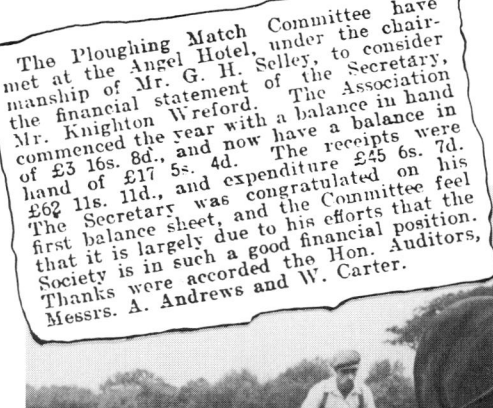

# PLOUGHMEN COMPETE AT WITHERIDGE

UNDER a cloudless October sky, expert ploughmen wrestled with abnormally dry soil at Witheridge, Thelbridge, East and West Worlington and Black Dog District Ploughing Association's 43rd annual competitions at New House and Essbeare Farms, Witheridge, on Tuesday.

For once, fine weather was a hindrance, and a cloud of rust-coloured dust hung over the competition fields.

Standards, however, were generally high, particularly in the digger classes. Roots were exceptionally good. Horse teams were outnumbered by tractors to the ratio of 25 to 3 This sextet—survivors of an almost extinct agricultural era—were, however, particularly fine animals, and worthy upholders of the reputation that Witheridge district has established of being the home of fine horses.

President of the association, Mr. D H. Amory, M.P., was among the visitors. Chairman of the organizing committee was Mr. J. Woolacott. Hon secretary was Mr. J. K. Mills and hon treasurer Mr. E. Cole.

Mr A. Beer is shown here competing in a ploughing match, one of the annual matches organized by the Witheridge and District Ploughing Association, whose history goes back as far as the 1820s. The matches are still held each year. Mr Beer started competitive ploughing at the age of seventeen, and didn't miss a match for over thirty years.

*Western Times*, 8 October 1948.

Of the two photographs taken at the ploughing match in the late 1940s one shows the straw and tarpaulin tea-tent with Mrs R. Rodd, Mrs J. Mills, Mrs J. Woollacott, Mrs R. Rowcliffe, Miss C. Selley, Miss P. Adams and Mrs W.S. Selley among those doing the tea. The group behind the flatpolls includes Mr R. Tarr, Mr J. Woollacott, Mr J. Mills, Mr T. Blackford and Mr Pugsley.

The Witheridge Tennis Club was founded before 1914, and played on three courts on rented ground behind the Manse, next to the Bowls Club. The two lady players in the pre-1920s garb are the Misses Constance and Vera Selley. The group was taken soon after 1925, the same year that Rev. J.A.S. Castlehow came to the village as vicar. The players are from left to right: Rev. Castlehow, Mrs C. Thorne, Mr W. Maunder, Miss R. Baker, Mr S. Thorne, Miss M. Thorne.

*Tiverton Gazette*, 11 June 1935.

## MORCHARD BISHOP v. WITHERIDGE.

Members of the Morchard Bishop lawn tennis club played their first match of the season at Witheridge on Saturday, June 1, and won by 109 games to 67. The scores were as follow :—

Mr. F. Edworthy and Miss Frost beat Mr. Maunder and Miss Selley, 6-5; beat Mr. Sillifant and Miss Adams, 10-1; beat Mr. Cox and Miss Maunder, 9-2; beat Mr. Thorne and Miss Williams, 6-5.

Mr. J. Burrow and Mrs. Mortimer beat Mr. Maunder and Miss Selley, 6-5; beat Mr. Sillifant and Miss Adams, 10-1; beat Mr. Cox and Miss Maunder, 7-4; beat Mr. Thorne and Miss Williams, 6-5.

Mr. W. Grant and Miss Horwill lost to Mr. Maunder and Miss Selley, 3-8; beat Mr. Sillifant and Miss Adams, 8-3; beat Mr. Cox and Miss Maunder, 9-2; beat Mr. Thorne and Miss Williams, 6-5.

Mr. R. Conibeer and Miss Mortimer lost to Mr. Maunder and Miss Selley, 4-7; beat Mr. Sillifant and Miss Adams, 8-3; beat Mr. Cox and Miss Maunder, 7-4; lost to Mr. Thorne and Miss Williams, 4-7.

The first Witheridge Bowling Club was formed in 1914. A notice in the *Tiverton Gazette* of 17 February 1914 reported that the Rev. J.P. Benson had presided over a meeting of the Bowling Club Committee at which rules were presented for discussion. They decided to get estimates for a pavilion, and to open their new ground after Easter. The 'new ground' lay at the back of the Manse behind the Congregational Chapel, and was leased. At a further meeting on 31 March, tenders for rolling and cutting the ground twice a week were considered, and the lowest, of £5-5-0 from Mr Fred Leach, was accepted. It was reported that the vicar had given timber for a pavilion and that Mr H. Way had offered to erect it for out-of-pocket expenses. In April, 80 people attended a dance in the Assembly Rooms, raising £2 in aid of the new Bowling Club.

In its history the club included a number of County players; among them have been Mr Frank Lawrence, Mr Francis Venner, Mr Dick Cox and Mr W.S. Selley. The photograph of 6 players was taken in 1928 and shows (left to right) Mr Joseph Leach, Mr F. Leach, Mr C. Leach, Mr F. Bryant, Mr G. Selley, Mr Crook. The group photo was taken at the opening of the pavilion. In the 1960s the ground was sold for development and the club closed.

*Tiverton Gazette*, 28 May 1935.

## WITHERIDGE

At a meeting of the Bowling Club, in the National School, the Vicar presided. The hon. secretary (Mr. G. H. Pullen) made a statement of the formation of the Club, and read letters from well-wishers, among whom were Dr. M. Cutcliffe (Dawlish), Messrs. Ian Amory, M.F.H., Cottrell (hon. secretary Tiverton B.C.), and W. Howe (hon. secretary Southmolton B.C.). It was decided that bonâ fide working-men of the parish should be allowed the use of the green during the evenings on the payment of 2d. The following officers were elected:—President, the Rev. J. P. Benson; captain, Dr. A. Houghton Brown; vice-captain, Mr. A. Andrews; Committee, Messrs. W. Carter, H. J. Mansfield, F. Maunder, W. Lee, and G. H. Selley, with Mr. G. H. Pullen as hon. secretary and treasurer.

*Tiverton Gazette*, 2 February 1914.

## TIVERTON v. WITHERIDGE.

At Witheridge on Saturday and won by the homesters by 38 shots. Scores :—

### TIVERTON

| | |
|---|---|
| A. E. Melhuish, L. Chaffey, C. Foss, C. Hamlin ... ... ... ... | 7—26 |
| J. Sharland, H. Bennett, G. Pengelly, W. J. Fewings ... ... ... | 22—12 |
| T. Dymond, R. Squire, J. Rawle, G. Purrington ... ... ... | 23—26 |
| C. Wood, E. Broomfield, S. Axhorn, J. Fewings ... ... ... | 9—35 |
| | 61—99 |

### WITHERIDGE

| | |
|---|---|
| C. Leach, J. Ford, J. Leach, F. K. Leach ... ... ... ... | 26— 7 |
| W. Rice, A. Bryant, T. Leach, F. Leach ... ... ... ... | 12—22 |
| H. Whitfield, B. Adams, F. Lawrence, E. Hutchings ... ... ... | 26—23 |
| F. Maunder, G. Selley, F. Balsen, L. Selley ... ... ... | 35— 9 |
| | 99—61 |

Witheridge Association Football Club was founded just after the 1914-18 war, and played on various fields before coming to rest on the present-day sports field. The photographs were taken in the early 1930s, and show the two teams turning out for a Married v. Singles match.

*Singles*
W. Rice
F. Bryant    G. Reed
F. Kingdom    W. Cox    J. Ford    C. Gard
S. Ford    A. Buckingham    R. Cox    C. Bowden

*Married*
F. Ford    W. Perry    C. Reed
W. Pyne    A. Bryant    J. Ford
S. Ware    F. Kingdom    L. Davie    B. Stemner    L. Baker

The Witheridge A.F.C. team photo of 1949/50 includes Mr F. Brewer, Mr D. Venner, Mr J. Payne, Mr L. Bourne, Mr W. Teague, Mr P. Tout, Mr J. Boax, Mr H. Tucker, Mr D. Southcott, Mr W. Burton and Mr J. Burrows.

Witheridge Cricket Club in 1946. The picture was taken at Chapner.
*Back Row*, left to right; J. Palmer, A. Cruwys, B. Johnson, S.R. Selley (Capt), W. Bond, M. Penfold, R. Lewis
*Middle Row*, left to right; A. Hill, J. Milton, R. Nott
*Bottom Row*, left to right; F. Clarke, J. Bryant, S. Osman, F. Godfrey

# WHIST MATCH

A whist match between 40 members of the Crediton District Constitutional Club and 40 from the Witheridge and District Whist Club took place at the Constitutional Club, Crediton, on Thursday evening, and resulted in a win for the Crediton Constitutional Club by 36 games to 24. Scores:—

### CREDITON CONSTITUTIONAL CLUB

| | |
|---|---|
| E. Combe and W. H. Whittington | 2 |
| S. Boddy and J. Phillips | 3 |
| F. Edworthy and R. Bailey | 2 |
| W. H. Baker and H. W. Davie | 2 |
| H. M. Phillips and A. Tonkin | 2 |
| E. Wyatt and H. Worthington | 2 |
| J. Reed and J. Dunn | 1 |
| A. Hammett and H. Madge | 3 |
| W. Staddon and W. Mitchell | 3 |
| S. V. Clarke and J. Westcott | 2 |
| F. Trott and A. Cox | 1 |
| M. Gregory and S. Staddon | 2 |
| B. H. Greenway and T. Clay | 2 |
| A. G. Hollis and W. Backwell | 0 |
| W. Doddridge and C. Ward | 2 |
| T. Reed and A. Grant | 0 |
| J. Rowe and H. Phillips | 3 |
| F. Dyer and W. Middleweek | 2 |
| J. Haynes and W. Southcott | 1 |
| W. Grove and E. Pollard | 1 |
| | 36 |

### WITHERIDGE CLUB

| | |
|---|---|
| Mr. and Mrs. Mansfield | 1 |
| Mr. and Mrs. Maunder | 0 |
| Mr. and Mrs. Andrew | 1 |
| Mr. and Mrs. Wreford | 1 |
| Miss Manning and Mr. Maunder | 1 |
| Miss Mansfield and Mr. Beardmore | 1 |
| Mr. Carter and Mr. Selley | 2 |
| Mr. Harris and Mr. Gunn | 0 |
| Mr. Burrow and Mr. Rogers | 0 |
| Mr. Saunder and Mr. Densham | 1 |
| Mr. Troake (2) | 2 |
| Mr. Daw and Mr. Hill | 1 |
| Mr. Travers and Mr. Vicary | 1 |
| Mr. Breyley and Mr. S. Selley | 3 |
| Mr. G. Selley and Miss Scoffham | 1 |
| Mr. C. Troake and Miss Wreford | 3 |
| Mr. Reed and Mr. Rice | 0 |
| Mr. Maunder and Mr. Lee | 1 |
| Mr. Trickey and Mr. Tonkin | 2 |
| Mr. Lee and Mr. Jones | 2 |
| | 24 |

Refreshments were afterwards provided for the visitors, and a pleasant evening spent.

## WITHERIDGE.

HORTICULTURAL SOCIETY.—A meeting of the Horticultural Society has been held in the National Schoolroom. Dr. Gordon presided. Mr. Mansfield reported the satisfactory balance of £13 19s. 4d. Messrs. Mansfield and Cornish, the hon. secs. having resigned, Dr. Gordon has consented to take the post. The Earl of Portsmouth was elected President for the year, and Dr. Gordon, the Revs. Buckworth and Benson, Vice-Presidents. Mr. Mansfield was elected treasurer, and the following Committee was appointed:—The Rev. S. Hill, Messrs. Butt, Churchill, R. Elworthy, R. Heywood, F. Leach, J. Leach, Delling, T. Partridge, Jones, W. Partridge, W. Tucker, E. Holmes, Yendell, C. Edworthy, F. Tucker, H. P. Cornish, Smyth and Denner. It was decided to add prizes this year for the best couple of fowls, ducks, and best two pounds of butter. The show will be held in the early part of August.

# WITHERIDGE FLOWER SHOW.

The 12th annual exhibition was held on Thursday and proved very successful, the exhibits numbering considerably more than 400. The Hon. Secretary is Dr. P. W. G. Shelley, and the judging was entrusted to Mr. Mairs (gardener to Sir John Shelley). The band of L Company 4th V.B.D.R., under Bandmaster Palfreyman, supplied the music.

# DINNER AND DANCE AT WITHERIDGE.

On New Year's Day the Witheridge Branch of the Rational Friendly Society held their annual dinner and dance in the National Schoolroom. The Vicar (Rev. J. P. Benson) presided, and was supported by Mr. L. G. Cruwys, Mr. Baldwin, Mr. W. W. C. Carter, Mr. Huxtable, Mr. Dart, Mr. H. Whitfield (Secretary), Mr. R. Cann, (Treasurer), Mr. H. Churchill, and over 30 others. Mr. C. Gunn, of the "Hare and Hounds," provided an excellent repast. On the removal of the cloth the loyal toasts were given by the Chairman.

Founded in 1822, The Witheridge Union Society existed to provide payments for medical attention, medicines and funeral expenses in all the parishes in Witheridge Hundred. Members had to pay sixpence a week, but funds were also raised by the annual Club Walk, which took the form of a procession on Oak Apple Day (May 29) round the village led by the band and the Club Banner. Girls wore a sprig of Oak Apple, but if they didn't, the boys pinched them! There were sideshows, roundabouts, swingboats, and a switch-back railway in the Square. People used to come from miles around and hundreds sat down to lunch in a marquee in Bell Close. The following is an account from the *Crediton Chronicle* of 1 June 1907:

# WITHERIDGE CLUB WALK

One of the most important days in the year at Witheridge is the one on which the Witheridge Union Sick and Funeral Benefit Society Club Walk takes place. Thanks to the energy of Mr. James Greenslade, who has been secretary for the past fifteen years, the Society was never in a more prosperous condition than it is at the present time, and last Wednesday's proceedings were consequently of a most successful character. When Mr. Greenslade first undertook the work the Club had a deficit of £30. Now there are 686 members, a deposit of £60 at the Bank, and a reserve fund of £309 6s. 6d. The receipts for the past year were £708 15s. 10d.

On the occasion of the Club Walk on Wednesday last the members marched to the Parish Church, preceded by the Society's banner and accompanied by the Witheridge Brass Band, under the conductorship of Mr. R. Southcott. The Vicar (the Rev. J. P. Benson) read the lessons, and the Rev. A. Du Pre, Rector of Washford Pyne, preached an appropriate sermon.

After the service the members formed into procession again, and marched to a field lent by Mr. George Selley, where a cold collation had been provided by Mr. C. Gunn. Upwards of 250 sat down.

*Crediton Chronicle*, 1 June 1907.

*Tiverton Gazette*, 5 January 1907

The annual dinner of the local branch of the Rational Association Friendly Society was held at the Hare and Hounds on New Year's Day. Dr. Meade presided, and was supported by Rev. J. P. Benson, Messrs. W. C. Carter, Dart, H. Whitfield (Chairman), H. Churchill (Secretary), F. Guscott, Crook, Wood (Committee), and others. Host and Hostess Reed provided an excellent spread. In proposing the toast of "Branch 601," the Chairman remarked that Clubs established for the mutual benefit of their members were most commendable. He coupled with the toast the name of their excellent Secretary. —Mr. H. Churchill, in reply, called attention to the fact that during 1905 fourteen new branches had been opened, and four of these were in Devonshire. Their branch now numbered 45, including honorary members. Their receipts had been £49 0s. 7½d. He had paid £6 10s. 8d. for medical aid, £19 9s. 2d. for sickness (the largest amount for some years), and had forwarded £19 0s. 4½d. to headquarters, leaving a small balance in hand.—During the evening songs were given by Dr. Meade, Mr. Hutchings, and Mr. Churchill. A dance afterwards held in the National Schoolroom was well attended, and a most enjoyable evening was spent.

*South Molton Gazette*, 11 June 1887.

JUBILEE CELEBRATION.—A public meeting was held in the National Schoolroom on Tuesday evening to decide upon the best method of celebrating her Majesty's Jubilee in the parish. Mr. G. Cutcliffe occupied the chair. Mr. G. Ayre proposed that a dinner should be provided for the men, and a tea for the women and children, but this not meeting with general approval, after some discussion it was decided that there should be a free tea, meat being provided for the men. The other item of the programme will be a special service in the Church in the morning, sports in the afternoon, and a concert in the evening, but the details of these matters have yet to be arranged by the Committee of Management. A suggestion, offered by Mr. Mansfield, to the effect that all surplus funds should be devoted to some permanent improvement to the town, was readily adopted by all present. For carrying out the necessary arrangements the following were appointed as a Committee :—G. Cutcliffe, Esq. (Chairman), the Rev. T. Torrens, the Rev. G. Bishop, Dr. Llewellyn, Messrs. G. H. Pullen (treasurer), C. Partridge, J. Partridge, Churchill, Sanders, Cornish, Mansfield, Besley, G. H. Pullen, jun., (Secretary), and A. Thorn. Also the following ladies:—Miss Cutcliffe, Mrs. Llewellyn, Miss Bazley, Miss Thorn, Mrs. Bishop Mrs. S. Partridge, Mrs. Cornish, Mrs. Sanders, Mrs. Mansfield, and Mrs. Besley. Among the donations received up to the time the meeting broke up were : — Mr. G. Cutcliffe, £5 ; the Earl of Portsmouth, £5 ; Dr. Llewellyn, £5.

*Tiverton Gazette*, 2 June 1908.

# WITHERIDGE CLUB WALK

The 29th of May is a great day at Witheridge. On that day for many years past the Witheridge "Union Society" has had its "Club Walk." This year glorious weather favoured the Club. From an early hour members and friends commenced to arrive on foot or in conveyances of all descriptions. The morning was spent in distributing the bonus and attending to various business matters on the part of the Committee and by saying "how d'ye do" to friends on the part of members generally. Punctually at noon the band struck up in the Square, and headed by the banner of the Society a tour was made of the principal streets of Witheridge. Arriving at the Parish Church a very large gathering crowded in to hear the preacher for the day, the Rev. Francis Hudson, of Chawleigh, who preached an eloquent and earnest sermon from the words : "Man goeth forth unto his work and to his labour until the evening." The preacher spoke of man's life, his labour and his limit, and very forcibly drove home the lessons of thrift as taught by such a society, and the still greater need of preparing for that hour when the limit of this life shall be reached by us all. A collection was taken on behalf of the Devon and Exeter Hospital.

After the service the procession was reformed and marched to a spacious marquee, the property of the club, in which nearly 300 members partook of luncheon. The Rev. J. P. Benson presided. At the close of the luncheon the report was read by Mr. Greenslade, the secretary. Various toasts were honoured—"The King," given by the Chairman; "The Bishops, clergy, and ministers of all denominations," proposed by Dr. Houghton Brown; "The preacher for the day," given by Mr. Greenslade; "The honorary members," proposed by Mr. Andrews; and "The Club," by Mr. Pullen. In responding the Rev. Hudson shewed that he could make a witty speech as well as preach a good sermon; and Mr. Cheney feelingly referred to the death during the year of Mr. Conner and Mr. W. Crook, two of the oldest members, and to the fact that Mr. John Leach, of Thelbridge Inn, who had not missed that luncheon for many years, was on his way to London to undergo an operation at St. Thomas' Hospital. The election of the Committee was proceeded with, and a very successful meeting was brought to a close.

The report was as follows :—Receipts— Balance in hand, May 29, 1907, £80 10s. 3d.; entrance and rules, £1 6s.; received as sick pay, £549 16s. 2d.; ditto as funeral, £58 7s. 11d.; ditto as fines, £8 10s.; honorary donations, £7 10s.; withdrawn from bank, £40; total, £750 6s. 4d. Disbursements.— Paid as sick pay, £489 18s. 4d.; ditto as funerals, £95; working expenses, £21 13s. 6d.; dividends to members, £138 11s. 8d.; balance in hand, £10 2s. 10d.; total, £155 6s. 4d.

*South Molton Gazette*, 2 July 1887.

## JUBILEE CELEBRATIONS.
*(Continued from our 6th page).*

### WITHERIDGE.

The celebration on Tuesday passed off most successfully. Nearly £45 was subscribed. Divine Service was held in the Church at 11 a.m., the Rev. J. Torrens preaching from Joshua iv., 20. The National Anthem was played by Mr. G. H. Pullen, jun., the organist, who supplemented it with the " Hallelujah Chorus." Shortly before 2 p.m. the school children, numbering 200, assembled and marched to a field (kindly lent by Mr. J. H. J. Partridge), where sports and amusements were provided. The arrangements for the tea were left to Mr. Brawn and Mrs. Whitfield. At 3 o'clock the juveniles assembled in the large marquee belonging to the Witheridge Club and had tea. Meanwhile the sports for adults were started, and the programme was gone through with marked success. Prizes to the value of about £5 were distributed. The Revs. Thomas Torrens and H. J. Bishop acted as judges, and Mr. Mansfield as starter. At half-past 4 the adults commenced to take their places at the tables, where they found a plentiful supply of boiled and roast beef, cake, &c., awaiting them. Altogether about 400 adults took tea. Dancing to music supplied by a string band, and the singing of the National Anthem brought a pleasant day to a close.

*South Molton Gazette*, 17 September 1887.

THE JUBILEE.—The Jubilee balance sheet showing a surplus of £7 9s. 7½d., a meeting was held at the National Schoolroom on Tuesday week for the purpose of deciding to what object the money should be applied. Mr. G. Cutcliffe occupied the chair. A proposition by Mr. Elworthy, Foxdon, to divide the money between the National and British Schools fell through, the unanimous wish of the meeting being to devote it to a fund for lighting the main thoroughfares of the town—an object that will alike be a fitting memorial of this year of Jubilee, and also prove a very desirable improvement to the town, whose streets now present anything but an inviting appearance on a dark night. For carrying out the decision arrived at by the meeting, a Committee was formed, consisting of the following members :—The Rev. J. Bishop ; Messrs. E. G. Llewellyn, Hill, Partridge, Johnstone, G. H. Pullen (Treasurer), H. Mansfield, Jas. Baker, Churchill, Mitchell, Brawn, and H. P. Cornish (Secretary).

Cups and saucers commemorating the Silver Jubilee of King George V and Queen Mary are being distributed in Witheridge Garage (which was also used for the Parish Tea) by the three oldest ladies in Witheridge; from left to right they are Mrs T. Tidball, Mrs Crook, and Miss Bodley. The little girl in white is Freda Selley, and the iron wheels of her sister Thelma's pushchair can just be seen with Mrs E.M. Selley sitting behind it.

The group picture was also a 1935 Jubilee occasion, and was taken outside the cottages in West Street (since demolished).

## WITHERIDGE

Jubilee Day celebrations were carried out at Witheridge in a right royal manner. Everyone seemed bent on enjoying themselves and the day passed off without a hitch. Householders had decorated the houses splendidly and the streets presented a very gay appearance. A service was held in the Parish Church conducted by Rev. J. A. S. Castlehow. Mr. J. Knight was at the organ. The church was full. A united service was then held in the Square by Rev. J. A. S. Castlehow and Rev. J. A. Hoyles (Methodist Minister, Cullompton), when a large number was present.

The procession then formed to march to the sports field headed by a band under Bandmaster J. Trevellyn. Children's sports were carried on in Mr. G. Selley's field until tea time, when the children paraded to the garage (kindly lent by Messrs. Greenslade) where each received a Jubilee cup and saucer which the three oldest ladies of the town, Mrs. J. Crook, Mrs. T. Tidball and Miss Crook, kindly consented to present. Tea for all followed, after which adult sports took place. Much amusement was caused, the pillow fights in particular causing screams of laughter, as also did the greasy pole, tug-of-war, wheelbarrow and tyre races and many other novel events.

A huge bonfire was lit in a field on Chapner (by kind permission of Mr. F. Tucker). A firework display was given. Community singing closed with Auld Lang Syne round the fire, and the National Anthem. The proceedings ended with a dance. The town was specially lighted for the occasion with coloured electric lights, even the flagstaff on the church tower being illuminated. Everyone thoroughly enjoyed themselves and Jubilee will not be soon forgotten at Witheridge.

*Tiverton Gazette*, 14 May 1935.

The wedding of Mr W.H. Bristow and Miss L. Lewis in 1913, and the picture is taken outside the cottage at Drayford where Miss Lewis lived. The bride and groom are seated; the bridesmaids in white are Miss K. Lewis and Miss P. Lewis. Left to right are: Mr Bill Thomas (driver and owner of the carriage), Mrs F. Squires, Mr Walter Bristow, Mr C. Squires, Mr H. Lewis (bride's father with beard), Miss H. Lewis, Mrs H. Lewis (bride's mother, without hat), Mr C. Lewis and Miss M. Lewis (fur hat).

Mr and Mrs W.H. Rogers ('Vigilo') on their Golden Wedding Anniversary in 1928. Vigilo was well known for his verses, which were often printed in the local papers. The following examples formed part of his report of the wedding of Mr Fred Selley, of Barton Hall Farm, Washford Pyne, to Miss Mabel Lee, of South Coombe in Witheridge.

*Tiverton Gazette, 28 February 1939.*

## WITHERIDGE WORTHIES

### SIXTY YEARS OF MARRIED LIFE

Memories of horse-drawn coaches, blizzards and rough roads are retained by Mr. and Mrs. Thomas Tidball, of Fore-street, Witheridge, who celebrated their diamond wedding on Friday. Mrs. Tidball is a native of Black Dog and was a Miss Amelia Chapple. Her husband hailed from Knowstone and they were married at Crediton on February 24th, 1879.

Mr. Tidball's first occupation was shoemaking. After marriage he and his wife moved to Leamington, eventually returning to Witheridge, where he took over his father's coaching business. Mr. Tidball's two sons were quick to take advantage of motor transport, and opened a garage. When Mr. Tidball retired from business his two sons joined with the two sons of a Mr. Thomas in the village and a few years ago, their firm became part of Greenslades' Tours Ltd., of Exeter, Mr. Fred Tidball being appoin-ted local manager at Witheridge.

At the family reunion Mr. and Mrs. Tidball, who are 82 and 84 respectively, were joined by their two sons, Mr. F. and Mr. W. Tidball, both of Witheridge, their two daughters, Mrs. N. Mantle, of Damp-ton, and Mrs. E. Phillips, of Bristol, their five grandchildren, and other relatives and friends.

Sally Brown got on her best gown
And forgot to peel the taters;
And old Jack Snell looked a regular swell
In kid gloves and new brown gaters.
Old Mrs Hall left the baby to squall
And hurried off to the Square,
And prim Miss Rice rushed off in a trice,
Forgetting to comb her black hair.
Said old Mrs Hyde, 'hers a brave sweet bride
As ever I zeed bloom,
And I'm bound to tell 'ee, Mr Fred Selley
Makes a downright manly groom'.
Old Farmer Higgs forgot his pigs,
For he meant the wedding to zee,
And dozens more from workshop and store
Out of respect for Farmer Lee.
To see the marriage we had a carriage,
And friends in the know said, 'thic's Vigilo,
A'driving with Varmer Hill'.

May prosperous times attend their farm!
   May beehives burst with honey! May heavy crops their eyesight charm!
May stock bring in good money! May she, when future years have fled,
   And children crowd the table, Feel no man equals Mr Fred,
And he, no wife like Mabel!

The parade of the entire cart horses at the Witheridge April Fair. This photograph was almost certainly taken before 1914, as by the end of the 1914-18 war Witheridge Fair and Market had been somewhat supplanted by Thelbridge as the more favoured locally.

The Spring Fair was always held on the last Wednesday but one in April, and farmers came in and paid their annual bills, often on the contra-account system. Children were let off school, and the tent outside the Angel contained one of the 'fairings' stalled where a sweet merchant from Chulmleigh sold his produce.

Occupants of houses used to barricade their windows on Fair Day on account of the horses.

A good deal of stock would go to Lapford Station; farmers on horseback with their dogs would drive bullocks, but lambs would be taken on flat-bottomed farm waggons with side rails to Lapford, where Mr Ernie Gunn and Mr Sid Snell used to kill under the 'dead arches' of the bridge and 'the train drivers used to come for the plucks', (livers).

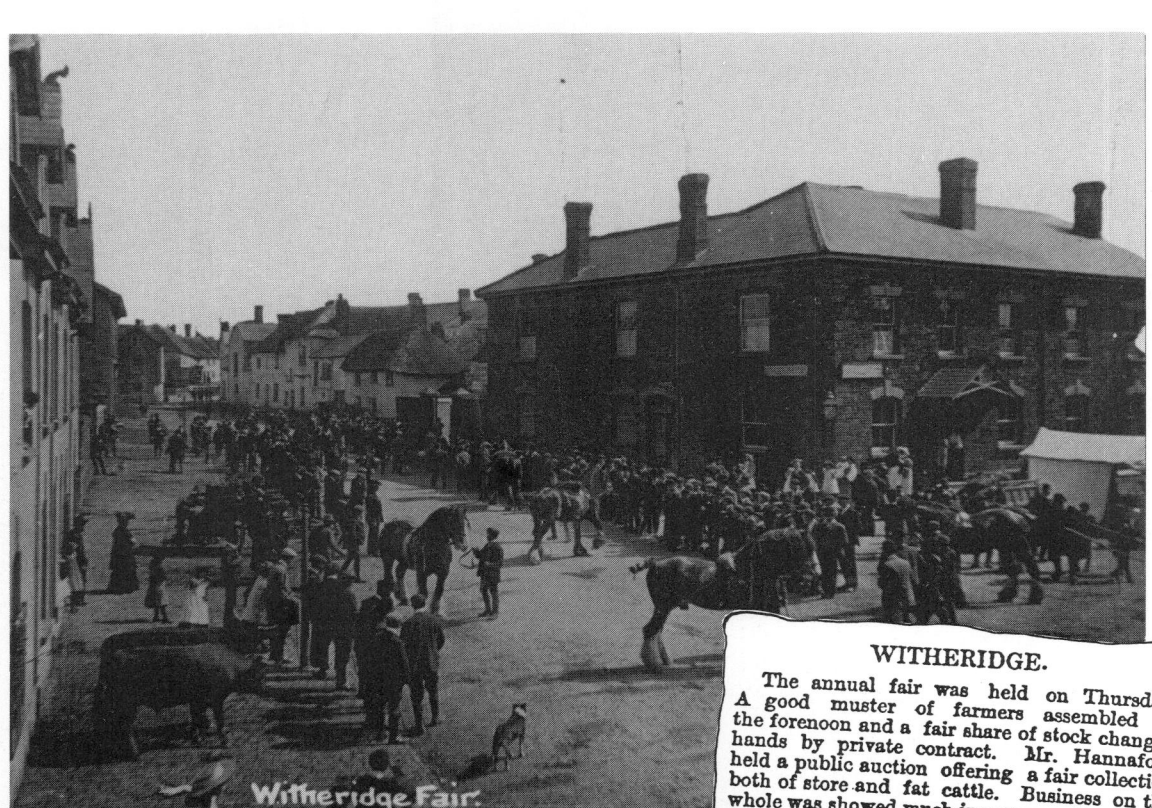

*Witheridge Fair.*

*South Molton Gazette*, 30 April 1887.

**WITHERIDGE.**

The annual fair was held on Thursday. A good muster of farmers assembled in the forenoon and a fair share of stock changed hands by private contract. Mr. Hannaford held a public auction offering a fair collection both of store and fat cattle. Business on the whole was showed much improvement upon last year. Perhaps Witheridge never before saw such a collection of amusements congregated in the square at one time, as were seen on Thursday last. The largest attraction was Bostock's Menagerie, which was well patronised, the daring performance of the lion tamer eliciting frequent applause. Smaller attractions of all kinds received their share of support and all seemed well pleased, both show-men and spectators. The village is to be congratulated on the absence of brawling and drunkenness, for in spite of the large gathering and numerous strangers, everything passed off pleasantly and harmoniously.

The hunt meets in the Square in the 1930s.

'Zaturday night at Jans' was the prizewinning float in the 1950 Witheridge Carnival. With the cups are Mrs Culhene, Miss Cannon, Miss Gloyn, Mrs Knight, and Miss Way; the musicians are Mr I. Nott, Mr K. Nott, Mr W. Blackford and Mr J. Bryant.

*South Molton Gazette*, 12 December 1887.

### WITHERIDGE RACES.

The Witheridge Races, which came off on Thursday, attained as high a degree of success as could reasonably be expected, considering the lateness of the season and the consequent uncertainty of the weather. As the latter turned out favourable, however, the course was in very good condition for racing, and the attendance was fairly large. The racing commenced shortly after 1 o'clock, the following being the events :—

PONY RACE (12.2 h.), one mile.—1st, Gregory's Flirt ; 2nd, Harris's Jane. Nine started ; very good race.

OPEN FLAT RACE for horses, 1½ miles. — 1st, Bucknell's Foxhunter ; 2nd, Harris's Emerson. Eight started.

FLYING STEEPLECHASE, 2 miles.—1st, Bucknell's Foxhunter ; 2nd, Jones's Game Cock. Five started.

BANKING STEEPLECHASE, 3 miles.—1st, Pope's Little Fairy ; 2nd, Tucker's Hawkridge. Most exciting race.

Darkness setting in at an early hour in the evening prevented the hurdles, galloway, and consolation races, announced on the posters from being run. The Witheridge Brass Band was present, and rendered in their usual efficient style a good selection of popular music during the afternoon. Refreshments were supplied by Mr. Jas. Baker, of the Angel Hotel, Witheridge, at which place the winners were awarded their prizes later on in the evening.

# WITHERIDGE CARNIVAL SUCCESS

## Splendid Entry in Colourful Procession

*Crediton Chronicle*, 28 October 1937.

### QUEEN CANDIDATES' GOOD WORK

### £58 from Penny Votes

For the first time since the inception of a Carnival at Witheridge, the torchlight procession on Thursday evening was headed by a Queen. She should have been an extremely proud monarch, for behind her was one of the finest and brightest convoys of originality, beauty, and humour that Witheridge and district has yet produced.

For some years past, Witheridge Carnival has enjoyed the reputation of being one of the highlights of the year in the district, and Thursday's eighth "annual" did much to enhance the reputation the event already enjoys.

Held under the presidency of Mr. John Yandle, the carnival was in aid of the Tiverton, Southmolton, and Devon and Exeter Hospitals, the West of England Eye Infirmary, and the Witheridge, Rackenford, Black Dog, and Cruwys Morchard Nursing Associations.

Organised by an energetic committee with the Rev. J. A. S. Castlehow as Chairman, the success of the event was greatly contributed to by the "spade work" put in by the hon. secretaries, Messrs. S. H. Hitchcock and B. Adams, and the hon. treasurer, Mr. W. Thomas.

'The Kings Messengers' was the name taken by these three little girls at a church concert in 1911. They are from left to right, Gladys Ford, Edith Bryant and Olive Baker.

A group has gathered in 1930 to celebrate the opening of the top playing field, which was provided through the generosity of Miss Mansfield for Witheridge and Thelbridge.

## WITHERIDGE WOMEN CONSERVATIVES

### ANNUAL NEW YEAR DANCE

Witheridge and Thelbridge Women's Conservative and Unionist Association's annual effort for funds always provides a good wind-up to the district's festive season. This year's effort, which took place at the Angel Hotel, Witheridge, on Monday night, was certainly worthy of the past tradition. The unqualified success of the effort was largely due to the energetic Hon. Secretaries, Misses Adams and Selley, who had the backing of an experienced committee.

Whist occupied the first part of the evening. Messrs. S. Selley and S. Ware were M.C.s and prizes were won by the following: Ladies—1, Mrs. A. Shapland; 2, Miss W. Chapple; 3, Mrs. Bowditch; 4, Mrs. Read; consolation, Mrs. J. Adams. Gents —1, Mr. E. Hutchings; 2, Mr. W. Bourne; 3, Mrs. W. Chapple (playing as gent); 4, Mr. S. Ware; consolation, Mr. C. Symes. Door stewards were Messrs. J. Adams, S. Selley and R. Rodd.

A fancy dress dance followed. Unfortunately only three patrons arrived in costume—a very poor response to the good prizes offered by the organisers. Prizes were awarded in the following order by Mr. A. Terry and Miss Mortimore (Divisional Agent and Organiser respectively): Ladies' costume—1, Miss Betty Way (Mad Hatter); 2, Miss Hilda Rowcliffe (Elizabethan). Gents—1, Mr. J. Churchill (Beer is Best). The engagement of the Excelsior Dance Band (Tiverton) ensured a crowded attendance and a pleasing programme, both of which fully satisfied the organisers and patrons. Mr. and Mrs. T. Ayre (Thelbridge) won a Victorian waltz contest and Miss R. Hunt and Mr. S. Coles (Rackenford) were the lucky couple in a spot dance.

*Tiverton Gazette*, 10 January 1939.

*Tiverton Gazette*, 15 August 1939.

## WITHERIDGE SCOUTS IN PARIS

### (From the District Commissioner, Rev. J. A. S. Castlehow).

Bank Holiday began the trip, when half-a-dozen Scouts and Rovers from Witheridge sunned themselves on the slopes of Old Sarum on their way to Southampton. This visit to Salisbury was just the prelude—a pleasant one—to a smooth crossing, and a rapid run through the orchards of Normandy, by the ripening cornfields, the stacks of hay and flax, and the neatly tethered cows, to Paris; where, at the Gare St. Lazare the boys were met by a French boy, Marcel Bushny, of the 5th Paris Troop of the Scouts de France, who escorted the party to his Troop H.Q. in the West End of Paris, near the Arc de Triomphe and the Trocadero.

*Tiverton Gazette*, 11 April 1939.

## . WITHERIDGE.

Considerable interest was taken in a crooning competition which was held during a novelty dance arranged by the Excelsior Dance Orchestra at the Angel Hotel, Witheridge, on Tuesday. The spacious ballroom resembled a radio studio during an amateurs' hour; there were several entrants who accepted the band's invitation to "mike" a name (or a noise!) for themselves. The following were the winners: Ladies—1, Miss Ivy White (Tiverton), who gave a splendid rendering of "Never break a promise;" 2, Miss Violet Bulled (Northmolton), who sang "So many memories." Gents.—1, Mr. J. Penfold (Rackenford), whose rendering of "My Own" displayed his perfect microphone technique; 2, Mr. Les Bourne (Witheridge), who sang "Mother Nature's Lullaby;" 3, Mr. M. Redwood (Rackenford), who rendered "Pocket full of dreams." Mr. Arthur Sharland was door steward, and Mrs. W. H. Buchanan was responsible for buffet arrangements.

## Witheridge Sale Of Work

A successful sale of work and jumble sale took place in the Methodist Schoolroom, Witheridge, on Thursday last. Rev. A. Law (superintendent minister) opened the proceedings. The stallholders were Mrs. B. Cox, Mrs. I. Kerslake, Mrs. Taylor, Miss A. Burridge, Mrs. R. Parkhouse, Mrs. W. Thomas, Mrs. H. Parkhouse, Mrs. Boundy, Miss Lemon, Miss S. Sowden, Miss J. Radford, Mrs. R. Tarr, Mrs. Pike, Mrs. J. Hill, Mrs. G. Sowden, Mrs. Parker. Brisk business was done and the Chapel Trust funds benefited by £35 16s 3d

*Western Times*, 4 June 1948.

The newspaper report appeared in the *Tiverton Gazette*, 8 September 1914.

The picture shows Sergeant Beer and the recruits about to leave for Tiverton in Tidball's brake.

Mrs Emily Williams' brother Bert used to go along and tap on Mr W. Greenslade's ('Billy Butterdabs') door and whisper, 'Bill, Bill, Kitchener wants one more man'.

Others in Witheridge were in the Yeomanry and had to report to Thorverton with their horses. They 'all thought it would be over in three months'. Later on, 'Mr Cruwys came buying heavy horses for the artillery, and farmers brought them into the Square for his inspection. He bought some and engaged men to get them to Lapford, including Mr Leslie Baker and his brother William who took three, each riding the middle horse'.

*Tiverton Gazette*, 9 May 1939.

## WITHERIDGE RECRUITING

### PLATOON OF 6th DEVONS FORMED

Over 20 men have enlisted in the 6th Devon Territorials at Witheridge, as the result of a recruiting meeting, and were sworn in over the week-end. A platoon has been formed. A special 'bus service to Southmolton twice a week has been arranged to carry the men to the training centre.

More recruits are expected, and it is hoped sufficient will be forthcoming to start a training centre at Witheridge. Mr. J. Churchill, the local recruiting officer, has been responsible for the arrangements.

The men of the 9th Battalion of the Manchester Regiment were billetted around the village in the summer of 1940. Their cookhouse was at the back of the Angel, and they ate in the big room upstairs. The Officers ate in the Hare and Hounds, and the NCOs were in the Mitre House. The presence of the troops, and the many evacuees, made the usual water supply problems so much worse that the army had to bring a water tanker to Witheridge daily; it soon became known as 'Gunga Din'. The W.V.S. ran a canteen in the Church Room and provided games, *Picture Post* and other papers, and a wireless for which they paid £8. So difficult were things for the army after Dunkirk that on one occasion there was no money to pay the troops, and a local man put up £300 as a loan to pay the Officers and their men their overdue wages.

The Manchesters were followed by the RASC and the RAMC, who parked their ambulances in the Square camouflaged to hide them from the German Bombers on their runs to Cardiff and Swansea. Later still the Royal Artillery came to Witheridge.

Witheridge Platoon Home Guard (photo taken in 1943 outside the Vicarage wall)

*Back Row (left to right)*
Richard Vicary, Jack Ayre, Geoffrey Hill, Bert Tucker, Stan Selley, Jack Adams, John Rowcliffe, Roy Cole, Harvey Boundy, Dennis Leat, Henry Beer, Donald Aplin.

*Middle Row (left to right)*
Bill Mann, Cecil Tapp, Eddie Partridge, Bob Woollacott, Ralph Tarr, Ted Gilbert, George Partridge, Alan Andrews, Sid Kingdon.

*Front Row (left to right)*
Frank Kingdon, Fred Gibbs, Jim Ford, Dennis Hill, Courtney Thorne, Colonel Phillips, Ned Ayre, B. Gibb, Percy Elston, Jack Stone, Archie Beer.

The Home Guard began in 1940 as the local Defence Volunteers (L.D.V.), whose uniform consisted solely of an armband. In addition to their training and more local duties the Home Guard also did searchlight duty at Venhay Down Cross at times to allow the army searchlight crew some relief. This point was on the German bombers route to Swansea and Liverpool, and it was the crews' task to hold an enemy bomber in its beam long enough for a fighter plane to shoot it down. At that time there were no anti-aircraft guns nearby.

When they started, their equipment consisted of armbands, shotguns and pitchforks. Later they were better armed, better than they knew on one occasion. One Sunday they were issued with live ammunition instead of blank without knowing it. 'We'd drawn ammunition for an exercise between two Home Guards over by Pedley and Stockham, and we couldn't understand why the others kept running away, until we saw the bushes and twigs being mown down, and a bicycle saddle pillar got shot through.'

The Witheridge war-time Fire Guard are at practice in the smoke hut built by Mr W. Vernon in the Market Field. They are dealing with a mock incendiary attack, having piled green grass into the shed and set it on fire to create the necessary smoke, through which they used to crawl one after the other practising rescue. Here Mr Stanley Price is pumping the stirrup pump, Mr Fred Darch is holding the nozzle, and Mr J. Leach is standing by the door. The gadget that Mr Darch is holding to direct the water on to the fire without danger to himself was invented by Mr Vernon. Produced in quantity in Witheridge by Mr W. Gold, the wheelwright and Mr J. Bristow, it was eventually adopted by fire guards throughout the United Kingdom as standard equipment for dealing with incendiary bombs, and may have saved many firemen's lives. Other members of the Fire Guard included Mrs F. Knight, Mrs Champion and Miss Keith. They were equipped with armbands, stirrup pumps, buckets and tin hats, although there were not enough to go round.

*Western Times*, 31 August 1945.

**WITHERIDGE**

VJ-DAY.—Witheridge was gaily bedecked with flags. A united thanksgiving service was held in the Square, Rev. J. A. S. Castlehow and Rev. R. W. Carr taking part. Fireworks were discharged at all points by the youngsters. Sumptuous teas were provided at the Assembly Rooms for the children and for all adults. Sports were held in a field, kindly lent by Mr. A. Tucker, followed by more fireworks and a dance.

TEA AND SPORTS.—A dance, held in the Angel Assembly Room, in aid of the Witheridge Welcome Home Fund, realized £8. For the free Victory tea, for the whole parish (about 500 people), the provisions were given, and in addition £28 8s 4d in cash collected towards the tea and sports, which followed in a field, kindly lent by Mr. A. Tucket. The day's programme ended with a dance, which realized £11 10s. The profit on the two days' events was £53 5s 7d.

This row of thatched cottages lay on the right hand side of the lane that leads down from the Church Room to Pullen's Row, and was known as Tracey Green.

In April 1945 the last of the big village fires occurred, and the Tracey Green cottages were the victims, together with the thatched cottages in West Street to which the fire spread. The village water supply was as usual inadequate, although many helpers did their best with buckets of water from various taps and wells. A number of fire brigades arrived, but no village source could feed the pumps – the vicarage well, reputed to be the best in the village, was pumped dry in three minutes. Water had to come from the river at Newbridge, and it took no less than six mobile pumps to relay the water up to the fire. It was all to no avail: Tracey Green and the West Street cottages were burnt out and never rebuilt.

# WITHERIDGE FIRE

## Cottages Damaged : Families Homeless

Six families were made homeless and cottages were destroyed at Witheridge on Tuesday in one of the worst fires the Tiverton district has known for many years.

Originating in one of a group of three thatched cottages at Tracey Green, the fire spread rapidly along the thatch to the other two and also to an adjoining two-storied house.

As the cottages blazed, a stiff easterly breeze carried sparks about 100 yards to ignite the thatch of a group of four cottages at Venn Bridge. All the cottages, five of which were occupied at the time, were destroyed.

The alarm was raised as soon as the outbreak was discovered about noon. Messages were sent to the N.F.S. and there were quick responses from several parts of the area. The firemen promptly went into action, running out threequarters of a mile of hose to the Little Dart river. It was soon obvious, however, that they were powerless to save the cottages, but they succeeded in limiting damage to the house.

Pending the arrival of the firemen, the whole village joined in salvaging the furniture. Most of the contents of the Venn Bridge cottages were saved, but the terrific heat at the other cottages prevented many of the household effects from being recovered.

Living with her father and mother at one of the Tracey Green cottages was a daughter who married only last week and lost practically the whole of the wedding presents. Her husband is in the Forces. Neighbouring cottages were occupied by Mr. and Mrs. Perry and their daughter-in-law, whose husband is also serving.

The Venn Bridge cottages were occupied by Mr. and Mrs. Woodhead, who were evacuated from Bristol; Mrs. Darch (temporarily living at Crediton), and Mr. B. Westcott and his daughter, Mrs. England, and grand-daughter. One cottage was unoccupied.

All the homeless were accommodated by relatives and friends in the village.

Among those assisting the firemen and in salvage operations were members of the W.V.S., Sergt. Fice, Con. Godfrey and Con. Beer.

*Western Times,*
27 April 1945.

Taken in the early 1900s this photograph shows Tracey Green, the long low set of cottages on the right, and in the middle of the picture are the 'stepped' thatched roofs of the West Street cottages which burned down with Tracey Green in 1945. The Church School is on the left.

This terrace of seven cob cottages with galvanised roofs lay across the present entrance to Appletree Close, parallel to North Street.

Mr and Mrs Frank Lawrence lived in No. 6 from 1932 to 1970 (the year of demolition), and the roofs were galvanised when they first went to live there. They were said to be snug dwellings, well protected from the north by the cob back houses against the street. There was one well at the front, but taps were also used between the end cottage and gunhole, and by the linhay at the entrance to Muxey Lane. Each cottage had a long narrow garden running towards what was then the 'doctor's paddock', belonging to the Firs: they were always beautifully kept, and much produce used to be sold. Other tenants included Messrs Partridge, Grant, Leach, Rice and Morrish.

The photographs were taken in 1969 as demolition started, hence the uncharacteristically unkempt appearance.

The narrow four-arch pack-horse bridge at Drayford had not been widened when the road on either side became part of the South Molton – Crediton Turnpike road in 1759, and the carts, carriages and wagons had to continue to use the ford beside the bridge as seen in the picture. One photograph shows the Adworthy Brook passing under a footbridge and joining the Little Dart. When the new bridge was built the Adworthy was piped under the road to enter the river below the new bridge. This enabled the creation of Drayford Green, where in 1919 Mr Harry Lewis planted four chestnut trees, ('one for each year of the war'). One of the original trees survives.

Drayford, Witheridge

92

In 1914 the bridge was replaced by the present structure, as an inscribed tablet in the downstream parapet records. A contemporary newspaper reported, 'Drayford Bridge is being replaced by a new one by Messrs Fothergill of Exeter. The present structure is an old pack-horse bridge "all up and down" in harmony with the surrounding landscape. It is not equal to the strain of modern traffic, and has latterly had to be supported by wooden posts. The new bridge is to cost over £1200'. All the children got an orange at the opening.

There was not universal support, however, and the Vicar refused to attend the opening and for some time afterwards, it was said, used to shut his eyes when he rode by.

DRAYFORD BRIDGE

The Chairman: The next thing is Drayford Bridge: we haven't heard the last of that yet—(laughter).

The Clerk read a copy of a letter addressed by him to the County Council and their reply. The latter stated that it was not the County Council's practice to pay contributions until the work had been completed satisfactorily, but in this case the Committee would possibly be prepared to depart from their usual practice, and the Council's letter would be placed before the Committee at their next meeting.

Mr. Drake moved that the Council proceed, and that Mr. W. S. Gardner be instructed to prepare plans to be submitted to the Bridge and Main Roads Committee.—Mr. Shapland seconded, and Mr. Maunder supported.—Mr. Jutsum thought that the plans should be sanctioned before the Council accepted the County Council's offer.—Mr. Drake concurred.—Mr. Drake's motion was carried.

*Tiverton Gazette*, 7 April 1914.

*Chulmleigh.*      Receipt No. 39032

# SUN FIRE OFFICE, LONDON.

RECEIVED *the* 1st *day of* June ----- 1891, *of*
The Earl of Portsmouth.    *the Sum stated at foot, being the Premium*
*for the renewal of the Insurance of* £ 6 4 0    *by Policy No.* 2 7 2 2 3 2 4.
*in this Office for one year from* LADY DAY, 1891, *to* LADY DAY, 1892.

*For the Managers of the Sun Fire Office,*

£ 1 : 12 : "

Stockham,
Witheridge.

\*.\* This Receipt to be used by Agents only.    Agent.

For many years, on the wall of the same cottage in Drayford that had the clockmaker's sign, there hung the sign of a sun, the badge of the insurance company known as the Sun Fire Office. This did not indicate that the company's agent lived there, but rather that the property was insured with that company.

A few yards south of the bridge was a cob and thatch cottage which still retained the sign 'Bradford, Clockmaker'. The Bradford brothers made clocks in Drayford from 1760 to 1808, when they moved to Tiverton.

Aerial view of Witheridge in the 1970s.

## ACKNOWLEDGEMENTS

We would like to thank the following people and organisations for all their help and assistance in compiling this book; Mrs. R. Alleyne, Mr W. Baker, Mr & Mrs A. Beer, Mrs Bourne, Mrs P. Bourne, Miss Bowden, Mrs G. Bristow, Mr A. Bryant, Mr C. Bryant, Mr F. Bryant, Mrs R. Buchanan, Mr A. Buckingham, Mr & Mrs Burgess, Mrs Carnochan, Mr F. Chapple, Mr & Mrs W. Churchill, Mr F. Davey, Mrs Densham, Mrs England, Mrs Gard, Mr T. Gibson, Mrs L. Gilbard, Mrs G. Greenslade, Mrs E. Heard, Mr & Mrs J. Knight, Mr & Mrs F. Lawrence, Mr & Mrs J. Martin, Mr K. Nott, Mrs S. Nott, Mr & Mrs E. Partridge, Mrs D. Payne, Mr W. Pyne, Mr & Mrs R. Reed, Mrs Rodd, Mrs M. Selley, Mr P. Smyth, Mr W. Stoneman, Mr & Mrs R. Tarr, Mrs W. Thomas, Mrs D. Tucker, Mr & Mrs F. Venner, Mrs O. Vernon, Mr A. Vernon, Mr H. Whitfield, Mrs E. Williams, Miss E. Winter, Mr & Mrs Woollacott, Witheridge Parish Council, Witheridge Fire Brigade, Lloyd Maunder Ltd, Notts Quarries, The Tiverton Gazette, Gordon Bray South Molton, Devon Camera Centre Exeter, Multiprint Tiverton and Devon Books, particularly Simon Butler and Julia Williams.